Faithful to the Lord

Faithful to the Lord

Compiled by
E. Stanley Williamson

BROADMAN PRESS
Nashville, Tennessee

© Copyright 1973 • Broadman Press
All rights reserved
4222-19

ISBN: 0-8054-2219-6
Library of Congress catalog card number: 72-97607
Dewey decimal classification: 248.6
Printed in the United States of America

Preface

The purpose of this book is to provide helpful concepts and illustrations for pastors and others who want their church members to truly understand the full meaning of stewardship.

In his sermon in this book, Dr. Morris Ashcraft uses this text from 1 Corinthians 6:19-20: "You are not your own: You were bought with a price. So glorify God in your body." He goes on to say in comment on this scripture, "This Christian concept is not only the basis of victory in life, but it is also the classic statement of Christian stewardship. Stewardship should always be defined in terms of man's total response to God—not just in terms of money." You will find this same idea basic to all the sermons in this book.

These twelve sermons have been prepared by some of the finest writers in the religious field, representing a varied cross section of background and experience.

John R. Bisagno, pastor, First Baptist Church, Houston, Texas

Cecil Ray, director, Stewardship Division, Baptist General Convention of Texas

Morris Ashcraft, professor of theology, Midwestern Baptist Theological Seminary

Bob Harrington, Chaplain of Bourbon Street, New Orleans, Louisiana

Charles G. Fuller, pastor, First Baptist Church, Roanoke, Virginia

William L. Self, pastor, Wieuca Road Baptist Church, Atlanta, Georgia

Charles L. McKay, pastor, First Baptist Church, Scottsdale, Arizona

Herschel H. Hobbs, former pastor, First Baptist Church, Oklahoma City, Oklahoma

J. D. Grey, former pastor, First Baptist Church, New Orleans, Lousiana

Harold C. Bennett, executive secretary-treasurer, Florida Baptist Convention, Jacksonville, Florida

Wayne Dehoney, pastor, Walnut Street Baptist Church, Louisville, Kentucky

R. Earl Allen, pastor, Rosen Heights Baptist Church, Fort Worth, Texas

A decided plus is the excellent illustrations included in each of the twelve sermons. They are warm-hearted stories that can easily be used.

These twelve sermons on the various facets of stewardship explore such areas as stewardship of influence, time, talents, the gospel, prayer, money, and vocation.

Many of our church members tend to identify the word stewardship with money. However, one sermon a month for one year on the various aspects of stewardship would be a wonderful way to lead church members to understand the true meaning of the work stewardship.

STANLEY WILLIAMSON
Director of Stewardship Development
Stewardship Commission,
Southern Baptist Convention

Contents

1. The Power of a Positive Influence   9
   John R. Bisagno
2. What's New About Tithing?   18
   Cecil A. Ray
3. You Are Not Your Own   28
   Morris Ashcraft
4. "It's All for Evangelism"—or Is It?   40
   Bob Harrington
5. The Priority of Prayer   45
   Charles G. Fuller
6. In the Interest of Time   55
   William L. Self
7. Witness Is for Now   62
   Charles L. McKay
8. Redeem the Time   74
   Herschel H. Hobbs
9. Love's Labor Lasts   84
   J. D. Grey
10. Go—Tell   94
    Harold C. Bennett
11. When God Hits a Dry Well   103
    Wayne Dehoney
12. In the Center of His Will   111
    R. Earl Allen

1

The Power of a Positive Influence

John R. Bisagno

Texts: 1 Chronicles 29:1–19; 2 Corinthians 1–9

Today we shall pledge $3,000,000 toward the $5,000,000 need to purchase the property whereon we stand and build the buildings necessary as a tool to do our part in winning this world to Christ.* Our "NOTHING IS IMPOSSIBLE CAMPAIGN" has been predicated on two simple truths:

1. Our inability to expand at the present church location.
2. The proper stewardship of our influence on other churches and on our world as illustrated in the two texts of the morning and that of our Lord himself on the cross. Let us review briefly both of them.

In the fact of near unprecedented church growth—nearly 3,000 persons have been baptized by this church in the past 32 months, in the midst of a city destined to become the largest city in North America in our lifetime—we are faced with the choice of stagnation or moving. Stagnation, because four simultaneous Sunday morning services are held at 11:00 P.M. in our present facilities and 14 Sunday school departments meet outside of the building, some as far as 3 blocks away.

Move, because no available land can be purchased at any kind of reasonable price in the downtown Houston area and vertical construction is a structural impossibility. So, the choice is clear. Stagnate or move.

* Sermon as actually preached by John R. Bisagno, resulting in a successful $3,000,000 fund raising campaign.

The new property to which we are moving is at the exact geographic and population center of our country. And, it is at the intersection of two freeways, receiving the highest exposure rate of any piece of property in the Southwest, with a third of a million cars a day.

During the lifetime of our Lord, he spent most of his time with a few key people, people whom he trained to influence the world for centuries after his death. History has not proven him to be unwise.

We stand here today because of the faithful stewardship of their influence potential.

Andrew Carnegie, that Baron of Iron and Steel, was asked what he would do if he lost his mighty empire. "Gentlemen," he said, "You can take my buildings, you can burn my factories, you can take away my wealth, but give me my key men, and I will build it all again." And that, ladies and gentlemen, is exactly how I feel about this near 2,500 persons gathered in front of me.

I believe you are the key to tomorrow. I believe that the influence of our church may well be an example which can help ignite world evangelism. I am not asking you to do simply what others do. I am not asking you to determine what you can give in light of a tax write-off. See in light of Calvary's sacrifice and in light of that great equalizer, the eye of God, which measures not so much what we give as what we keep for ourselves.

The theme of this entire campaign has been the stewardship of influence—being good stewards of what each of us has, not what someone else has, but what we have. The theme is not equal gifts, but equal sacrifice. And, our staff, our teen-agers, our single young adults, our seminary students, and our advanced gifts committee have each made exemplary sacrificial group pledges as good stewards of their influence to challenge and inspire the rest of us to do our part. And that is exactly what I am asking of you—that you do your part.

One day during the peak of World War II, a group of coal miners came to Winston Churchill. Discouraged with their seeming unimportant lot in life, they demanded to volunteer to go to the front and fight. The next day a meeting was arranged in Royal Hall, and Winston Churchill arose to address the 4,000 miners in attendance. "Gentlemen," he said, "They say he is coming," referring to Hitler. "They say he has 100,000 men on the sea, 100,000 on the land, and 100,000 in the air. But, I say to you that one day we are going to be victorious over this matter and one day we will walk down the streets of London in victory and I will say to a young soldier, 'Where were you in Britain's finest hour?' And he will answer, 'I was in the trench with my rifle fulfilling my responsibility, doing my part for my country.' And, I will say to a wife and mother, 'Where were you in Britain's finest hour?' She will say, 'I was in a hospital caring for the wounded, fulfilling my responsibility and doing my part for my country.' And I will ask some of you where you were during Britain's finest hour and you will say, 'I was down in the pit of the mine with my face against the face of the coal, fulfilling my responsibility, doing my part for my country.' "

Ladies and gentlemen, I say to you this morning that we are going to be victorious over this goal. One day we shall walk down the streets of Houston as the world is blessed by the influence of this great soul-winning church, and I will say to a little paper boy, "Where were you in the First Baptist's finest hour?" He will say, "I was giving 50¢ a week throwing newspapers, doing my part for First Baptist Church." I will say to a college student, "Where were you in First Baptist's finest hour?" He will say, "I was working at that part-time job, giving $4.00 a week." I will be saying to you who will be pledging $20, $50, $100, or $1,000 and more, "Where were you in First Baptist's finest hour?" And, you will do well to say, "I was down to the bed rock pit of my ability with my face against the face of my responsibility, doing my part for First Baptist Church." And, the faithful exercise of each of you shall bring about an unbreakable chain of commitment which shall ultimately bring about the victory we so earnestly desire for our Lord.

The text we have read from 1 Chronicles described a seemingly impossible victory of contribution which ultimately made it necessary for the King to plead with the people to stop bringing their gifts because far too much had come in. And the reason is found nestled in verse 3 where King David, faithful in the stewardship of his own influence, set the example and precedent by giving all of his own private treasure.

The story in 2 Corinthians is again a story of the ministry of the influence of stewardship. The people of Macedonia, gave out of great poverty, to the people of Jerusalem, who were undergoing great famine. Paul used this as an illustration and example to the church at Corinth to admonish them to do as well. And, the key is in the fifth verse, which says this amazing thing: They were able to do more because they "FIRST GAVE THEIR OWN SELVES TO THE LORD."

So, as you exert an influence on others by your pace-setting pledge, you yourself in so doing, illustrate the influence that has been showered on you by others. Let us remember that it is not first of all your money that your Lord wants, but you yourself. THEY FIRST GAVE THEMSELVES.

The principle of the surrendered life before the act is one with which the New Testament is repleat. Jesus said when the disciples warned and pleaded with him to eat, "I have meat to eat that ye know not of. My meat is to do the will of him that sent me." And, again in the Sermon on the Mount, "Not everyone that saith unto me, Lord, Lord, will enter the kingdom of heaven; but he that DOETH THE WILL of my Father which is in heaven." Again, in the Garden he pleaded, "If it be possible, let this cup pass from me: nevertheless, not my will, but thine, be done." It is only a surrendered will which makes possible the existence of the stewardship of our influence in the sacrificial pledge. THEY FIRST GAVE THEMSELVES.

Jesus warns that if we have aught against our brother, we must leave our gifts at the altar and go make peace, or the gift will not be received. And, Paul adds that the Lord's Supper is not to be observed until we are in accord with one another. THEY FIRST GAVE THEMSELVES.

I would suggest three simple reasons why they were able so to give.

First there was an unselfish motive.

Well has it been said that Christianity is a cross, and a cross is "I" crossed out. No one word more adequately expresses the thrust of the whole Christian gospel than the word "others." In the eleventh chapter of Acts, Agabus had prophesied of famine to come upon Jerusalem. Here in Corinth the example of the Macedonian believers, themselves in poverty, is used to influence the Corinthian church out of much abundance to do half as well.

The motive of need in giving to others has always been used in Scripture. Jeremiah and Isaiah both responded to God's call when he broke their hearts with the vision of an unclean people in whose midst they dwelt.

Moses cried to God for deliverance because of the need of his people in sore bondage down in Egypt. And, even our Lord himself . . . so loved the world . . . that he gave. Here we are 2,000 years later, we who shall continually be an influence to others, being influenced by them. For there is no greater motivation to the unselfish giving of our influence than the motive of love, evoked by the needs of others.

Second, they gave out of an unimagined influence.

Never did they imagine or dream what their example was going to be. No father can imagine how much his son will become like him. What little girl does not ever-so-naturally begin to walk, talk, and act like her mother. We are creatures of influence— we humans. We live not to ourselves. We die not to ourselves. Whether we live or die, we influence other people.

A few months ago I wrote a little book entitled *How to Build an Evangelistic Church*. IN THESE INTERVENING WEEKS, NEARLY 6,000 PREACHERS HAVE BOUGHT COPIES OF THAT BOOK, AND UNCOUNTED NUMBERS HAVE WRITTEN TO SAY IT WORKS. Oh, the influence, dear church, that you exert on our world as First Baptist, Houston, casts her long shadow across Christendom.

In our lifetime it is said that Houston will become the capital of a megalopolis, stretching in crescent-like fashion from New

Orleans to Corpus Christi. Need I remind you that in this space capital of the world, while our Lord is making more people, he is not making more space. Here, to Houston, men by the millions are coming. And, what will they find? For one thing, we know that they will find the eighth wonder of the world, the Astrodome. It is my dream because of the influence and example you shall exert when you sign those pledge cards today that they will find the ninth wonder of the world as well—the winningest, the givingest, the ministeringest, the lovingest, the caringest church this world has ever known. A church where our children and their children's children, if our Lord tarries his coming, will stretch the shadow of their influence from this mighty citadel of evangelism round the encircling globe.

Those Macedonian believers never dreamed the dimension of influence they would have on us here today. Nor, have we touched the hem of the garment when we try to imagine the influence that this church can have upon our world for years to come. They gave from an unselfish motive and, indeed, they gave as well from an unimagined influence.

Third, they gave from unexceedable example—that of the influence of our Lord himself. Listen again to the ninth verse of that passage. "For ye know the grace of our Lord, that though he was rich, yet for your sakes he became poor, that ye through his poverty might be rich." Rich! And, oh, how rich we are in him! And why? Because he gave himself, willingly and completely on the cross, totally and completely, without reservation, suffering indignation, enduring every infliction for us. Isaiah records that he was wounded for our transgressions. Medical science tells us that there are five basic kinds of wounds, and the Gospel writers affirm that he bore them all.

1. The contusion—a bruise inflicted by the striking of a blunt object endured by Jesus as he was beaten by the fists of brutal men.

2. The laceration—a jagged, tearing wound endured by Jesus with the scurge of the whip.

3. The abrasion—a wound created by a tearing or shreading by the twisting and rubbing of the thorns which crushed his brow.

4. The puncture—a piercing hole created by the nails in his hands and his feet.

5. The incised wound—an incision created by a sharp object, inflicted by the spear in his riven side.

But, while the example of our Lord Jesus enduring all pain is used by Paul as an encouragement to influence us to give all, still these were not the deepest wounds that Jesus suffered. I speak of the psychological wounds, the wounds of his heart and spirit, for those surely hurt the most.

1. The wound of denial—Peter, of all the disciples, had been the most privileged. It was he who made the great confession at Philippi. It was Peter who was privileged to go to the Mount of Transfiguration in the highest hour of Jesus' glory and into the garden at the deepest hour of his need. And when the young maiden said, "You are one of his. I know you are for I have seen you with him and you talk like him." Peter swore and said, "I know not the man." And Jesus turned to look at Peter. The eyes of the big fisherman met his own, and Peter's denial broke the heart of Jesus. Yes, Peter spent all the rest of his days saying, "I know him. I know him." But, he never forgot the night he denied the Lord and said, "I know him not."

2. But, Jesus was wounded with *the wound of materialism* as well. Wounded by Judas of Kerioth, the only disciple who did come from Galilee. It is my thought that Judas was so much like the Christian businessman of today. He had two main interests in life. He had a religious interest. He memorized the decalogue. He went on missionary journeys, he kept the treasury, he accompanied the disciples. He had a genuine interest in the things of the kingdom. But, Judas had another interest—a material interest, an interest in making money. And, the time simply came when it came into conflict with his religion. He was forced to make his choice. But, before you are too hard on Judas, ask yourself the question, "What am I actually willing to financially sacrifice these next three years for the sake of my religion—in the name of my Christ?" For do not most of us under the same circumstance act as did Judas?

3. There was the wound which hurt the most—*the wound of*

silence. Jesus was tried in two courts—the religious court of Jerusalem and the political court of the Roman Empire. He was found guilty in both. But, there was one court of appeal which occurred only to Pilate, a man who was so troubled, so convicted, so convinced of the innocence of the Nazarene, that he went to the final court of appeal, the court of public opinion. As was the custom on the Feast Day, the people were given the right to obtain by choice the freedom of one man. And, to the last man the unanimous consent of the people was, "Release unto us Barabas. Away with this Jesus. Let him be crucified!" When it was all on the line, not one in the crowd spoke in his defense. Where were the lepers he had healed and Lazarus he had brought from the dead? And, Mary Magdalene, whose sins he had forgiven? Where were his mother and faithful disciples? They were in the crowd. They owed him so much. But, not one raised his voice in his defense. He was condemned to death, condemned by the silence of his friends. Silence . . .

During the reign of Julius Caesar, mightiest of the Roman Emperors, a plot arose in the Roman Senate to assasinate him. The date was set for the fifteenth of March, 44 B.C., a date which has come to live in infamy, a date known as "the ides of March."

On the eve of the fatal day, Caesar's wife, Calpurnia, awoke him at midnight, screaming in terror. She had had a vision in the night of his assasination and begged him not to go to the Senate the next day. "Go back to bed, foolish woman. You have only had a nightmare. These people are my friends. They love me. They would do me no harm."

The next day on the way to the Senate a soothsayer yelled from the crowd, "Go not to the Senate today for there you will die. It is "the ides of March." "Away, child of hell," cried Caesar. "These people are my friends. They love me. They would do me no harm."

Amid a flurry of congratulations, hand shakes, and warm smiles, Julius Caesar entered the Senate. Suddenly, Casca, a Roman senator, thrust a dagger into his back. Then, the other senators were upon him, wounding him again and again with their daggers. The last and final blow was thrust into his abdomen. Looking down at his bleeding stomach he saw the dagger, the hand and the face of his best friend, Brutus. Silence gripped the Senate. "You too, Brutus," he cried. "Then die, Caesar!"

History records that 24 wounds were inflicted upon his body. But, the fatal blow came from the hand of his best friend.

Zechariah 13:6 records, "And one shall say unto him, What are these wounds in thine hands? Then he shall answer, "Those with which I was wounded in the house of my friends." The wound of silence, the silence of his friends, was the fatal wound to Jesus.

You are here today because you are his friends. You love him deeply and because you love his bride, the church. Today you have the opportunity to speak more loudly than you may in all of your life. To speak with your influence, to speak with your love, with the signing of a pledge card. We are here because of the influence of others. We shall influence other yet unborn millions for him because this day we who are his friends shall speak and speak loudly in his behalf.

2

What's New About Tithing?

Cecil A. Ray

Texts: Acts 20:35; Mark 12:43–44; Luke 19:8; Matthew 9:15–17.

The Christian is called to a *new* life in Christ. In Christ the new life explodes into a pursuit of new ways to live, new demands for living, and new satisfactions from living. Yet it remains that the Christian must live in a world of the "old" and thus he faces the constant issues of the *new* and the *old*. Jesus illustrated this by saying, "Ye have heard that it hath been said by them of old time . . . but I say . . ."

The devoted follower of Jesus will look carefully at the value and meaning of the old but will always relate himself to it in light of his new life in Christ. It is in this light that the Christian should ask "What's *new* about tithing?"

Tithing itself is old. As a practice of giving it dates back into antiquity. It seems to have begun as a spontaneous act of giving designed to show recognition and honor to one's deity. It was practiced by the peoples of many religions. In the early history of Israel, under the leadership of Moses, the tithe became a law. This law, although often changed, set the tithe as a legal and thus compulsory, standard of giving.

In this particular study of the *old* and the *new,* the old is identified as the law of the tithe. The early simplicities of a spontaneous act of worship were replaced by a complex legal tithing system.

What's New About Tithing?

In Deuteronomy (read Deuteronomy 14:22–28; 26:12; 12:6–17) three tithes were specified calling for at least 20 percent or perhaps 23 percent, depending upon the interpretation of the third year tithe. The tithing system changed during the course of Old Testament days and even in the days between the Testaments, so that by the time of Jesus it had become an intricate maze of ritualistic laws. Some accounts indicate that there were as many as twelve different tithes required by Jesus' day and that this amounted to as much as 40 percent giving.

The "new" in this study is what Jesus Christ started. Christ did not simply patch up the old religion with some new ideas, he gave men *new life*. In Matthew 9:15–17, Jesus talked of the folly of putting new patches on old garments or putting new wine into old containers. He did not give men a new life simply to have it bottled up in old law or bound by old traditions.

It is at this point of understanding that the Christian can begin to find meaningful answers to "What's new about tithing?" The practice of giving for the Christian is not and cannot be simply a continuation of the "old" law. What giving is all about for the Christian must be answered from the perspective of his new life in Christ. It must find its definition, motives, purposes, and measure of "how-much" from Christ. This makes the understanding of the issues involved in the *old* law of tithing and the *new* spirit of giving most vital.

These issues are important in helping the devoted follower of Christ come to understand the distinctly Christian meaning of giving. Involved are:

The issue of attitudes. If the attitude is "how little can I get by with?" or "do I have to tithe?" it is not Christian. The attitude of the Christian is "how much can I possibly do for my Lord?"

The issue of life-style. The life of the Christian is not lawless, but it is shaped by Christ rather than by law. It is a life ruled by Christ as Lord and filled by the indwelling Spirit.

The issue of motive. Love motivates the believer, and, in turn his giving must rise from this love rather than from the compulsion of law or the fear of punishment.

The issue of quantity. Christ's 100 percent giving is the goal of the believer. In fact, how much he actually gives is set by how seriously he responds to Christ as his Lord. He will benefit and learn from the law of the tithe. It must be noted that at no point in the Old Testament is the tithe a simple 10 percent of one's total income. It varied from 20 percent to 40 percent in its application and touched chiefly the agricultural and animal products. It did not include the income of the tradesman and craftsman. Therefore, the tithing system of the Old Testament cannot simply be transferred over into the life of today's Christian and be enforced. However, the principles taught in tithing are important to the Christian.

The issue of rewards. The Old Testament individuals were frequently encouraged to *tithe* in expectation of material reward. By contrast, the expected reward of the Christian is the satisfaction of serving his Lord and helping accomplish his work.

Jesus did not come to destroy the *old*—but in his own words he "came to fulfill the law." It is his fulfilling the law that sets the whole new scheme of life into action. He takes the old and replaces it with new meaning and new purposes. In doing this, it is apparent that Jesus did not elect to talk much about the old tithe. He refers to tithing on two occasions—and this only as a side issue to the point of discussion (Matt. 23:23, repeated in Luke 11:42 and 18:12.) He does, however, talk much about giving. Acts 20:35 records Jesus' basic perspective—"It is more blessed to give than to receive." He exalts the giving examples of the widow (Mark 12:41–44; Luke 21:1–3); the woman with the alabaster box (Matt. 26:6–13); and the good Samaritan (Luke 10:25–27).

Jesus condemns wrong attitudes and motives in giving (Matt. 6:1; 23:23; Luke 18:12; Matt. 15:5; and Mark 7:11.) He gives instructions on giving (Matt. 6:2; 19:20–22; 25:36–46; Matt. 5:23; Luke 19:1–9.) From these specific references and from the total of Christ's message can be found valid principles to guide the Christian in giving.

In the light of Jesus' teaching on giving it is imperative that

Christians reevaluate their attitude and views about tithing. It is well to ask: "Is it good for the Christian to tithe?" The answer is *yes*! The answer is *no*!

It is *yes*—if

(1) tithing is adopted as a guide to assure a good foundation for giving;

(2) tithing is practiced as a recognition of God's ownership and the believer's responsibility to God for all that he possesses.

(3) tithing is an act of love.

It is *no*—if

(1) tithing is viewed as being the full obligation that the Christian has (like paying a debt in full);

(2) tithing is keeping a law for the sake of reward;

(3) tithing is practiced as an excuse to escape other responsibilities to God;

(4) tithing prevents one's growth in greater proportionate giving;

(5) tithing is motivated by fear of God's reprisal or punishment.

At this point it may be well to start calling the Christian's approach to tithing the *new tithe*. When tithing is presented as a guide for the Christian it should be in this new sense. What is meant by the "new" tithe is illustrated by the Sunday School teacher who stated last week, "My tithe for this next year will be 15 percent." He was using the word "tithe" to describe his promised gift as a Christian. This was not an example of a man responding to a law, but a man following a good principle and growing in his love for Christ.

The spirit of the "new" tithe will bless a Christian. It is in this way that the Christian finds tithing to be a great blessing. It helps him as it serves:

(1) as a guide to proper acknowledgments;

(2) as a model for giving, and,

(3) as a start in proportionate giving.

Tithing Prompts Acknowledgments

Tithing is founded on the idea of acknowledgment.

The tithe began as a voluntary and spontaneous gift. It seemed to be a generally accepted expression of one's way to honor God. The worshipper gave the tithe as his acknowledgment of God's ownership of all things and as an expression of gratitude. This spirit was evident in the early law period in the form of a celebration of the goodness of God. The tithe has undergone extensive changes in the course of Israel's history, but only in its abuse has it lost this original idea of response to God.

Three tithes were called for in the early Levitical law (Deut. 14). These are listed by Dr. Richard Cunningham of Golden Gate Baptist Theological Seminary as the celebration tithe, the charity tithe, and the Temple tithe. This tithing system and its subsequent developments provided funds for a mixture of causes including religious work, charity, government, and even war.

Obviously, this complex tithing system (and it grew even more complex) cannot be the guide for today's Christian. However, the principles behind this system do remain valid and very important as a guide.

Tithing reminds the giver of God's ownership.

When the Christian chooses to honor God with the gift of a tithe as a love response to Christ, he finds that it invariably reminds him of the fact that God owns everything he possesses. He learns anew that not only the 10 percent given is God's but the other 90 percent as well. Israel was not permitted to forget (see Deut. 8:17–18) her dependence on God and was admonished, "Beware lest you say in your heart, 'my power and the might of my hands have gotten me this wealth,' you shall remember the Lord your God, for it is he who gave you power to get wealth."

It is urgent that today's Christian not be permitted to forget this same truth. With the coming of affluence has come also the grave danger of selfishness and of undue preoccupation with the accumulating of material possessions. Prosperity has an uncanny capacity to turn a Christian's thoughts and concerns to himself. Instead, prosperity should awaken new commitments of giving and service. It should be an occasion when the Christian claims prosperity as an opportunity for taking great forward steps for his Lord. This note of deep commitment should be the note sounded in our response to the "new" tithe.

Tithing points the believer to God's great purposes.

Giving, even great acts of sacrificial giving, are not ends within themselves but are to be linked with the great purposes of God. They are to be expressions of the will of God in the believer's life. Many times, however, the believer is first led to tithe and then, in so doing, comes to see his giving as truly a part of the Christian life. It is then that giving becomes more than a response to the economic needs of the church. Such an experience leads the believer to see himself in an exciting partnership with his Lord in a worldwide redemptive enterprise.

The spirit of the "new" tithe (as it is used in this sermon) is one of response on the part of a Christian who has learned the meaning of giving from his Lord. God is the great giver—and it is from his giving that the follower of Christ understands the motive, the amount, and the purposes of giving. The ideal is for the Christian to let God's giving be expressed through his giving. As this happens, the Christian captures a lofty sense of purpose for his life and giving becomes a very personal expression of commitment.

Giving and one's relationship to Christ are inseparably linked. To give is to reflect this tie with Christ. What Christ does in the life of the redeemed sets in him a new life with giving as a part of its character. To cultivate and develop this "inherent" response is to become more like Christ. To neglect its development is to thwart the will of God.

A dramatic example of this spirit of the "new" tithe was experienced by this writer while pastor of the Arnett-Benson Baptist Church in Lubbock, Texas. It happened when the church was just beginning. The deacons were frequently divided on important issues, and this threatened the future of the church. It became apparent that generally the divisions over issues were between those who were tithers and those who were not. As the reality of this dawned upon the tithing deacons, they met and agreed to pray for and witness to the other deacons about their Christian giving.

In the following six months many visits were made and much prayer offered. God blessed the efforts and suddenly the church had a revived group of deacons. Many commitments were made and 100 percent of the deacons began tithing. Dramatic changes in attitudes resulted. A new marked ability to work together was realized and the church began to experience growth.

Tithing Provides a Model for Giving

Tithing guides to accomplishments.

"A model is important because it provides a visual or mental image which enables men to accomplish desired goals." Worthy accomplishments are not accidental, and accomplishments in the field of Christian giving are no exception. Success comes from the ardent pursuit of goals. Worthy goals or models serve to keep the individual's objectives high and also to serve as a gauge in measuring progress. For one individual progress may involve growth away from occasional or spasmodic giving toward regularity. For another, it may involve growth upward from a 1 percent, 2 percent, or 4 percent giving practice. Whatever the past practice, worthy goals lead to growth. The follower of Christ, who is sincere in his profession, will find great benefit in adopting the tithe as a model for giving. It will guide him into a workable and systematic way of reflecting his love to God.

For the Old Testament man the tithe was a legal obligation. By contrast, the Christian finds the tithe to be one very helpful model in learning how to discipline himself in the distribution of his material possessions. The fact is, the believer will find the tithe to be a good teacher in getting started in the grace of Christian giving.

Tithe-giving helps link the believer to Christian concerns.

When a Christian joins a church he becomes a part of a community of believers. This is a covenant community, where individuals bind themselves together for worship and for service to Christ.

In becoming part of this fellowship the individual surrenders his autonomy to the congregation in whose life he shares. He remains responsible for his actions yet works to support the objectives of the group. Through fellowship and giving he is linked in joyful sharing in the life and work of this church-family. The concerns which Christ has committed to his people then become the individual's concerns.

A certain deacon learned the joy of such sharing. At the time I first came to know him, I learned that he was seldom pleased with his church and its work. Then suddenly his whole attitude changed, in fact, so noticably that it was observed by his fellow members. One day he said, "I guess you have noticed a change in me. Well, I'd like to tell you about it." He continued by explaining that his outward negative attitude was a reflection of his inward unwillingness to honor God with his money. This change, according to his own testimony, came when he adopted the tithe as his beginning standard for giving. The greatest benefit resulting from his decision was his concern for his church and his devotion to the ministries of the church.

Tithing helps the believer set priorities.

A good model or goal pursued by an individual helps him in determining priorities. When a Christian declares, "I can't give as much as the tithe," he is usually reflecting his priorities in life. In essence, he is saying, "I have my priorities (my wants in life) so arranged that such giving is impossible." Tithing serves to help set priorities in order because it leads to an acknowledgment that God is first, and that Christ is the Lord in every area of one's life.

Tithing Teaches Proportionate Giving

Tithing is a practice in proportionate giving.

To tithe is to give a tenth part. In the Old Testament the tithing system called for a series of tithes as a legal obligation. The New Testament continues the principle of proportionate giving but changes the spirit of giving from a law to the impelling grace of God. This is particularly evident in the Apostle Paul's admonition: "Upon the first day of the week let everyone of you lay by him in store as God hath prospered him, that there be no gathering when I come" (1 Cor. 16:2).

Two mistakes have characterized many modern Christians in their relationship to the tithe. Unfortunately, some have missed the Christian meaning by trying to impose the Old Testament legalism of the tithing system. Equally unfortunate have been the reactions of others who, in wishing to be free of any sense of obligation, have completely removed the tithe. Both have missed the true meaning of giving for the Christian. Giving that has its basis in Christ is free, generous, and even lavish, never selfish. Jesus spoke openly and freely about giving. In fact, he made giving an expression of Christian living. It is at this point that the practice of tithing can help the believer learn.

Tithing begins a search for greater proportions.

Tithing is a good model for giving. It is not the only model, nor is it the greatest. Joy comes to the follower of Christ as he sees new options in his giving and as he adopts greater models and goals. Some believers have started their growth in giving by adopting the 10 percent goal and moving steadily toward it each year. Others have found the tithe actually to be a sacrificial proportion and one that calls for very deep commitment to Christ. For a host of other believers the tithe can only be worthy as a beginning point, and, for them, meaningful commitment calls for higher goals.

Jesus dealt with the subject of giving always by holding up great examples and by setting lofty goals. Acts 20:35 records Christ's keynote on the subject, "It is more blessed to give than to receive." He sets the cornerstone for building the Christian life-style. He gives his followers additional insight into what giving is all about as he acclaimed the gifts of the widow (Mark 12:41–44; Luke 21:1–3). She gave all she had. This basic principle of giving is better illustrated by the 100 percent giving of Christ himself. Here, it is well to underscore, that when one's eye is on Jesus, even though the tithe can be used as a helpful model, his real goal will be to be like Jesus. One who has his eyes on Jesus will never call any percentage, be it 8 percent, 10 percent, 20 percent, 30 percent, 60 percent, too much. He will never complain that any giving is impoverishing.

Somehow, it is not really Christ's kind of giving to get by with as little as possible. The idea of God's grace in one's life is not an excuse for covetousness or selfishness. It does not prompt one to seek freedom from responsibility. When a Christian expresses these attitudes, it is evident that he has misunderstood what following Christ is all about.

For the sincere Christian, it is neither the question of "how much," nor "how little." He will long for the growing capacity to achieve new goals—goals of 15 percent, 30 percent, 50 percent, 80 percent. He will match his longings with actions. It was this kind of longing plus the fervent glow of the Spirit of God in their lives that moved the early Christians to sacrificial giving (see Acts 2:44–45; 4:36–37.)

Such longings continue to possess many believers' hearts today. Douglas Brown, Secretary of the Church Stewardship Department in Texas, encountered just such a Christian. It happened a few years ago while he was visiting in behalf of the giving-commitment day in his church. One member assigned to him was a very poor widow. Knowing of her circumstances his first impulse was not to stop at her house.

Brown decided, however, to stop just to visit, but not to ask her to give. To his great surprise the woman was expecting the visit and was ready with her commitment card. Her poverty had not robbed her of a great spirit of giving. His inclination was to encourage her to keep this for herself. "Now, young man," she said, "you must not take this privilege away from me." He left there with the glowing experience of having seen a great Christian whose eyes were on Jesus and who saw no gift as too much or impoverishing.

3

You Are Not Your Own

Morris Ashcraft

Texts: 1 Corinthians 6:19–20, 4:2.

A young college freshman discovered the true meaning of Christian stewardship almost accidentally. He was attending noon-day devotionals during a time when he was struggling with bad habits and temptations. His home life had not been Christian; he had been converted only a year or so before; his life was unstable. The devotional thought for the day was our text, "You are not your own; you were bought with a price. So glorify God in your body." (1 Cor. 6:19–20). This thought came as a revelation to him. He later testified that in times of struggle he recalled this inspired thought and gained victory over his temptation. He was reminded, "I am not my own. I belong to God. I must live for him!" This Christian concept is not only the basis of victory in life, but it is also the classic statement of Christian stewardship. Stewardship should always be defined in terms of man's total response to God—not just in terms of money.

But, material wealth and the understanding of it are very important. Its possession is necessary; its potential for good or ill is almost infinite. The greedy quest for it and the cruel misuse of it have resulted in such human suffering that many pious souls have renounced it with vows of poverty. And yet, God is the Creator of things. And, therefore, things are good in themselves. We have used them for evil. How can we correct our misuse of them and use them for good? This is our subject today. We have defined *stewardship*; we must now define *responsible*.

The word *responsible* helps to clarify the meaning of Christian stewardship. The basic requirement of stewardship is found in Paul's statement, "Moreover it is required of stewards that they be found trustworthy" [faithful], (1 Cor. 4:2). This could well be translated, "It is required of stewards that they be found responsible."

A responsible person is one who (1) responds to the persons and needs around him (2) on the basis of his own understanding or interpretation of these demands (3) as an accountable person who is willing to accept the consequences, immediate and ultimate, for his decisions and actions. I am indebted to H. Richard Niebuhr, the late distinguished professor of ethics of Yale Divinity School, for insights into responsibility. Niebuhr's analysis appears in his posthumous volume, *The Responsible Self*, 1963. A chapter of that book, entitled "The Meaning of Responsibility," has been reprinted in a volume entitled *On Being Responsible*, edited by James Gustafson and James Laney.

The emphasis on responsibility is very helpful in overcoming the legalistic emphasis in ethics. Teachers of ethics have long recognized the inadequacy of legalism, but the oversimplifications of "situation ethics" likewise left much to be desired. Niebuhr's emphasis on responsibility is a very helpful alternative. It goes without saying that stewardship teaching and preaching have tended to be legalistic. But, Jesus constantly fought against legalism. Paul struggled to keep Christian faith free of its stranglehold.

Christian stewardship should be conceived in terms of intelligent responsibility, never in terms of legal requirement. We shall be concerned, therefore, with stewardship which is responsible. This means: (1) A Christian must *respond* to God, fellow man, and self and to the needs around him with his total self including his material possessions: (2) He must respond in terms of *his own considered interpretation* of possessions, talents, opportunities, and needs: (3) He must be *accountable* to God, others, and self for his decisions and actions.

Convictions of Responsible Stewardship

As Christians we bring certain theological beliefs with us to our decisions. These beliefs provide a part of the basis for understanding responsible Christian stewardship. A brief reminder of these convictions includes the following ideas.

God is Creator. We read Genesis 1:1 with the accent on *God.* "In the beginning *God* created the heavens and the earth." God is first. We affirm our belief that all else, (heavens, earth, etc.), owes its existence to him. We affirm that the creation, therefore, owes its origin, nature, and purpose to God. It forever remains dependent on him, while he forever remains God, independent of, and sovereign over, creation.

Our knowledge of God comes from his revelation in Jesus Christ. "In the beginning was the Word . . . and the Word was God . . . all things were made through him . . . and the word became flesh and dwelt among us" (John 1:1-14). "In him all things were created, in heaven and on earth . . . in him all things hold together" (Col. 1:16-17).

We therefore, believe that God our Creator is due our total response in faith and devotion, and that our lives and use of his creation must please him.

Man is creature. The biblical view of man is sharply distinguished from all other views. Man, in the Bible, is always seen first as God's creature. Man bears God's image, but is not divine. Even fallen, estranged man bears God's image and is therefore redeemable. Man is forbidden to kill or injure other men because they bear God's image. Men must care for their fellowmen, because all are creatures of God. But, man stands between God and other creatures.

Man has dominion. Man is never merely a creature along with other creatures. He has power and sovereignty over nature. While he must never seek to usurp the powers of God, he must subdue and rule over nature. However, he must always account to God for the exercise of his dominion, and he must live with the consequences of his reign.

When man turns against God, whether prompted by pride, sensuality, or unbelief, he disrupts the harmony in nature and the fellowship with other men. He changes dominion over nature into exploitation of it. It responds to man's sin with "thorns and thistles." When man rejects his responsible dominion, he turns creation into a hostile world. Man must return to responsible stewardship.

The earth is the lord's. Our tenure on earth is short! Threescore and ten, perchance fourscore years! Our lease of the land is temporary. When political powers are stable we may be able to bequeath portions of the land to our offspring, but in time all leases revert to Him who holds the title to the land. Every voice in creation cries out that man must die. Only God goes on! But, while we live, we can live for God. All the more reason for being responsible stewards of the earth which is forever the Lord's (Psalm 24:1)!

Responses in Responsible Stewardship

The gospel of Jesus Christ is the good news that God has not disowned us, but has moved to redeem us. It awakens within us the memory that once we belonged to God, indeed we can belong again. It arouses the hope that our inheritance is not forever lost. God calls us back to our intended role as creatures of God—to responsible stewardship.

Not my own. The estrangement and loneliness from being away from God gives way to a new belonging. Paul said it perfectly, "You are not your own." Not my own? Then whose am I? In modern times we have been overly concerned with the question of identity. Our concern has been alloyed with a measure of self-centeredness and a lot of insecurity. Man asks, "Who am I?" The best way to put the question is, "Whose am I?" Let me illustrate.

It happened the day I left home to go to college. My father was a poor man, but an honest and respected man. We had a large family—eight children. The depression which began in 1929 left my parents in very difficult circumstances. We all worked. We were very happy, and together, but poor.

My father was not able to provide the money for my college expenses. With some embarrassment, he acknowledged this fact as he spoke to me the day I left. He told me that I was free from family responsibility if I could find a way to earn my college expenses. Then, he said to me, "Although I am not able to send you to college, I let you go with a good name. I have given you a good reputation. There are no scandals associated with your family name. And wherever you go I want you to remember *whose son you are.*" I've never forgotten, and it has made a difference.

Jesus Christ calls us back to God and lets us know "Who we are" by first reminding us of *"Whose we are."*

Bought with a price. But, our return to God was very costly. Jesus Christ died on the cross to bring us back. Paul compared it to slavery which threatened every man who lived in the biblical world. Conquering armies often defrayed the expenses of war by selling their captives. One could be emancipated if someone would pay the purchase price. Paul reminds us that we were slaves to sin and that Christ set us free. Now we belong to God in a two-fold way: he created us, and he redeems us.

What it means to belong. Were you ever the "new kid" in a school? Did you ever stand outside some desirable event or circle of persons without being invited in? On the other hand, have you known the warmth and sense of purpose derived from belonging to such a group?

In our time we have so stressed a kind of distorted freedom that we may have lost some of the meaning of genuine belonging. We belong to our families, to our church, to our country. To be sure, there are some groups to which we should never belong, and we should never belong totally to any except God.

For instance, Dietrich Bonhoeffer was a German during Hitler's regime. He loved his country and belonged to it. But, he did not belong totally to his country; he belonged to God first. When the choice was forced, he chose to stand for God. It cost him his life, but today we know that he loved his country more than those who "belonged" totally to it. A man must not sell his soul to the company store, but man cannot live without belonging. Life's meaning is found in belonging.

A young aircraft pilot during World War II told of an experience which illustrates the meaning of belonging. Like many other young men, he took dangerous and unnecessary risks just for "kicks" by flying too near the ground, trees, and bridges, etc. Seemingly, he had not grown up; he had parents, brothers and sisters, and a wife. He owed them enough to be careful with his life, but he did not think of it. He later told that he grew up one day while engaged in such an illegal and dangerous maneuver.

While in inverted flight in a plane not designed for it, he suddenly thought of his wife and their child expected in a few weeks. It dawned on him that he was very foolish to risk the life of the father of an unborn child. He terminated the maneuver and "grew up" into a responsible man instantly. He learned that belonging to others, even to one unborn, gives meaning to life and alters one's behavior.

The loyalties of life may conflict, and man must find a way to relate them. The Christian believes that by belonging to God first, he can keep other claims upon his life in a manageable harmony.

Glorify God in your body. "To glorify" means to reflect back to God his own holiness. We bear the image of God; he wants to see it when he looks at us. "Body" means more than physical body; it means the whole personality. To glorify God in the body means to respond to him so openly and fully that one's life becomes a mirror in which God's image is reflected back to him. God is Creator; he expects us to be creative. God loves; he expects us to love and care for our fellowmen. God forgives and redeems; he expects us to learn the redemptive power of forgiving others. God is sovereign over the universe; he expects us to exercise responsible dominion over our small plot of creation. God owns all things; he expects us to manage our material possessions in a way that is responsible.

The Practice of Responsible Stewardship

Christian stewardship involves one's entire life; it is just as important to use one's time, abilities, influence, etc., properly as it is to use wealth properly. There are several New Testament teachings on the responsible use of wealth. But, the first response is personal.

A personal response. In the practice of responsible stewardship of material possessions, one must respond first with personal decision. It cannot be legal or material. First, I must give myself. The apostle wrote, "I seek not what is yours but you" (2 Cor. 12:14). Paul was correct when he insisted that we must give ourselves to God before we can practice responsible stewardship of things. But, in the passage cited, Paul was apologizing to his readers because he had not permitted them to provide for the financial support of his ministry while he was among them.

Paul had spent his time making tents to support himself, and took pride in supporting himself. In doing so, he had prevented the Christians at Corinth from being responsible in supporting the ministry. He wrote, "I have been a fool! . . . Forgive me this wrong!" They were irresponsible in stewardship; Paul felt partly responsible.

Legalism tends to become impersonal. Christian faith insists on personal response, repentance, faith, commitment. One cannot become a Christian by subscribing to the faith of his fathers; he must repent and believe for himself. In the stewardship of possessions, he cannot be responsible by obeying a law inherited from the past. He must think it over, make his own response—himself.

Legalism offers security and comfort; it relieves man of the task of deciding on a personal basis. But, legalism is sub-Christian. From the very beginning in the New Testament and throughout Christian history, the temptation to legalism has been evident.

It is particularly tempting in stewardship. In our time, tithing has been substituted for Christian stewardship and is next to a "requirement" in many circles. The case has been built on Jesus' statement in Matthew 23:23, and stated that Jesus endorsed tithing, or set it as a minimum, as the correct giving percentage for Christians. The fact is that Jesus was condemning the scribes and Pharisees for their diligence in tithing while neglecting the "weightier matters" such as "justice, and mercy and faith." Christian stewardship is first of all the personal giving of the whole self.

This should not be understood to mean that personal response means less materially than legal response. In all probability it means much more. The Christian cannot meet his standards with 10 percent; he must dedicate all he is and has to God. When it comes to deciding how much he will "give" to his church, he may decide to do much more than 10 percent.

A considered response. We have insisted that a decision or action is responsible only if the person has reflected on his decision and has made it in the light of his own convictions. *"Each one must do as he has made up his mind,* not reluctantly or under compulsion, for God loves a cheerful giver" (2 Cor. 9:7). This statement does not mean that "one interpretation is as good as another," nor does it suggest "the right of private judgment" in so far as the meaning of Scripture is concerned. It means that one cannot engage in responsible Christian stewardship until he has taken an inventory of his own life, including possessions, and responded to God in terms of his own faith.

One must give, if he gives at all, for the right reasons. For instance, it would not be Christian stewardship, though one may give liberally, if he is motivated by the desire for publicity, in order to gain power in the congregation, to avoid taxes, or out of fear.

"Cheerfulness" in giving must involve many factors, but certainly the main idea is that of giving out of conviction. It must not be "an exaction but as a willing gift . . . not reluctantly or under compulsion" (2 Cor. 9:5–7). The cheerful giver is the one who gives liberally as "he who sows bountifully" because he anticipates that he "will also reap bountifully" (2 Cor. 9:6). The cheerful giver is not the one who gave little; rather, he is the one who gave bountifully for the right reasons. At least, Paul said, "The point is this" (2 Cor. 9:6).

A proportionate response. The New Testament does stress proportionate giving, but it refuses to state a fixed percentage. However, there are two guidelines which help us to decide our proportion: (1) our ability to give, (2) our assessment of the need and creative opportunity for giving.

Giving according to one's ability to give, "as he may prosper" 1 Cor. 16:2) has long been accepted as a fair standard. We avoid the exploitation of those who are not able to give. But, this does not necessarily mean that we can agree on an exact percentage for each to give, such as 10 percent before taxes. Within a given congregation, members may agree upon some minimum, or standard, as a guide and may use it well in the development of stewardship, but there are dangers. We may forget to appraise our own ability to give. We may settle for less than responsible stewardship. We may exact from others a percentage which they have not agreed upon in their own minds. We may re-establish legalism.

Preoccupation with the right proportion of income tends to hide the other aspect of proportionate giving. When we assess the needs, or causes to which we give, there is the imaginative faith of some which enables them to give liberally as one "sowing bountifully." They visualize or anticipate what can be achieved by the Christian dedication of their material possessions. They give in proportion to their faith and in excess of the proportion set by their earning power.

A school teacher in a large city in the western part of the United States illustrates this kind of stewardship. Having no family, she spent relatively little on her own needs. She customarily gave between twenty and thirty percent of her income directly to her church.

Even on the small earnings of a public school teacher she managed to invest small sums in the purchase of land. As the years passed, the value of the land increased until she had a relatively large estate. Although she died in middle age, she had already given considerable sums beyond her church contributions to supplement the salaries of mission pastors and missionaries, and she left a significant amount of wealth to worthy causes. She had dedicated all of her radiant life to God by helping people in material ways. She achieved responsible stewardship in proportion to her joyful faith, not in proportion to some "fixed" percentage.

A consistent response. "On the first day of the week, each one of you is to put something aside "(1 Cor. 16:2). Regular giving may be once a week for some, once a month for others, annually for farmers and the like. Regular giving is a necessity in our age. Those of us who share in the life of a church congregation have united our resources and efforts in a Christian ministry. We know how necessary it is to plan and spend systematically and regularly. We help to determine what the ministry will be and how much it will cost. We project our estimates of expenditures and we pledge ourselves to be good stewards by regular giving. It would be completely irresponsible if we failed to keep faith with our Christian brothers and sisters who also share the responsibility.

An accountable response. The Christian glady accepts the fact that he is accountable to God both now and ultimately. But, are we not also accountable to ourselves? Am I not accountable to my own conscience? Am I not also accountable to my fellow Christians? Accountability does not have to do with publishing information about our giving, nor even with keeping good records of our stewardship as advantageous as that may be for income tax purposes. It means accepting responsibility for the consequences of stewardship. It means that I am answerable to my fellow laborers for bearing my share of the load.

For instance, the minister is answerable to his congregation to live according to his teaching. As a teacher, I am accountable to my students to live in accordance with my theology. This accountability does not imply that someone calls me in as a subordinate (that, too, is a kind of accountability) to explain. It means that we have joined in a common effort; we have shared the faith together; we have walked side by side in the Christian venture. We belong to each other and must be answerable to each other for our faithfulness. This is genuine responsibility.

But accountability does not end with responsible giving; we are also accountable for the use to which our gifts are put. Money is power. It has great potential for good or ill. The giver is accountable to see that his gifts go to their intended purpose and that the purpose is right. It is just possible that money given to our churches may end up in selfish and wasteful spending. Don't many churches spend most of their money on their own comfort and enjoyment? Is that responsible? How much of the church budget actually gets to distinctively "Christian" ministry?

It is possible that one may respond liberally to appeals for money, say by radio religious programs, for good causes, only to learn later that he was defrauded, that he contributed to a charlatan. Is that responsible stewardship? Of course not! One is accountable. He is responsible to take precautions and to be sure that material possessions given for Christian causes actually get there. It may be necessary to attend business meetings of the church or to serve on the finance committee. Paul was accountable in stewardship. He took double precautions: he required accrediting letters to accompany funds; he also required messengers (1 Cor. 16:3-4).

To be responsible stewards we must dedicate ourselves totally to God. Then, we must evaluate all of our resources and dedicate them to God. We must respond to God and to human need in the light of our own growing appreciation of the privilege of sharing with God in his work. In the realm of material possessions, we must use all in a way that will honor God. The only way we can do this is by our genuine care for fellowmen. We must dedicate specific gifts to God's work among men in proportion to our ability, our creative faith, and the needs of our world. We must give regularly and adequately to those causes which deserve our support. We must be accountable both now and later for our stewardship.

One of the most forceful and responsible presentations of Christian stewardship I have ever heard was given by the chairman of a finance committee in a Baptist church. The church was located in the growing part of a large city. The members were, for the most part, young families. They had come together and dedicated their efforts toward having a distinctive church in their area.

It was a vigorous congregation with an enthusiastic and capable long-range planning committee. The church had a vision of the future and worked toward it.

The chairman appealed to his fellow church members, "We have united our lives and efforts in the work of our church in this community. We have already accomplished some significant goals, we have agreed to increase our efforts and dedication. We have made pledges to God and to one another. After thorough discussions, we have adopted a budget which represents our best planning for the coming year.

"Now it is up to us to underwrite the budget. Only by so doing can we accomplish the ministry we have planned. No one else is responsible for paying for this ministry; it is ours; we planned it; we are responsible for it. We should not expect others to pay for it; we should not spend or plan to spend on the basis of what we expect others to give. This is our responsibility. I appeal to all of us to be responsible."

"It is required of stewards that they be found responsible." Let us be so responsible that some day the Lord will say to us, "Well done, good and faithful steward. You have been responsible!"

4

"It's All for Evangelism"—or Is It?

Bob Harrington

Evangelism is the most important thing we do. Isn't it?
No, it isn't!

The most important thing we do is what we spend the most time doing and give the highest priority. That rules out evangelism.

In the early '60's, you will remember that a number of Baptist state conventions were using the slogan, "It's All For Evangelism." I recall one state in particular that used this slogan on every piece of promotion for three years. Brotherhood—It's All For Evangelism; Cooperative Program—It's All For Evangelism. This convention made it perfectly clear that everything it did was really for evangelism.

After three years, here was the result: the state showed gains in every area—more in Sunday School, more money, more in W.M.U., more leadership awards.

What about evangelism? During the three year period, the churches baptised 1,000 less each year than the year before!

Everything gained but evangelism—and yet, it was all for evangelism!

We are notorious, as Christians, for doing well in everything but the one thing we were called to do—win people to Jesus Christ.

Evangelism Is First with God

We better get something straight—evangelism is first with God, and it better be with us.

I recall the story of the lighthouse keeper. He had one job—to keep the light burning. He even had an emergency vat he could use in case the main vat ran out of fuel.

One day there was a knock at his door. A man in a motor boat was out of gas. The lighthouse keeper felt sorry for him. He took some fuel out of his emergency vat and gave it to the man.

The next day he had another caller. Someone else needed fuel. He had heard how kind and helpful the lighthouse keeper was.

The lighthouse keeper became the most popular man in the community. They made him president of the Chamber of Commerce. He became known as the most benevolent man in town. Everyone knew that if they had trouble and could make it to the lighthouse, they were in safe hands.

Late one night there was the sound from a ship in distress. The keeper awakened to see the light going out in the tower. He raced down the staircase and switched the turncock to the emergency vat. It was empty! That night a ship crashed on the rocks at the foot of the lighthouse.

It made no difference that he had helped many people in lesser ways. The fact was that a ship crashed because he had failed to do the one thing he was there to do—keep a light reaching out into the darkness.

There are many things a Christian can do to help his fellow man. And there are endless little things a church can do for people. But there is only one thing that Christians have been called to do before all else and above all else—keep the light of the gospel reaching out to a world in the darkness of sin.

Evangelism is first with God, and it better be with us.

Evangelism Is First with the Christian

You may be doubting what I have said up to this point. I can hear some of you saying, "It may be true that some Christians are supposed to witness, but I think we all have different talents. It may be that God expects some of us to do the witnessing and others of us to do the other chores that need to take place around the church."

There is only one thing wrong with this line of thinking—it is a lie born of the devil! The devil would be the happiest one in hell if he could convince Christians that only some of them were supposed to witness. The next thing he would do is convince the ones who were witnessing that they were only supposed to do it part of the time. This is why Christianity is so weak today. We have listened to the devil instead of God for our commission and have ended up with a minority group of God's "half-witnesses."

Let me ask you a question: why do you think God left you on this earth after he saved you? You are now his child, and he isn't going to let you go. You now have a home in heaven, waiting for you. Why doesn't God go ahead and take you to heaven, since we all agree it is going to be better than what we have on this earth? I'll tell you why God has left you on this earth—for one reason and one reason only—to help take other people to heaven with you!

When I first surrendered to preach, I tried to get to the bottom of what makes some of the great men of God tick. Billy Graham said that he only wanted to be one thing—an effective soul winner. Dwight L. Moody said that he only wanted to be one thing—an effective soul winner. Therefore, that's what I decided I was going to be.

When I opened up my office on Bourbon Street, I got a number of reactions, and all of them were bad. People in general thought I was after a fast buck and a loose woman. Other ministers thought I was a sensationalist. The folks on Bourbon Street thought I was a nut. I can tell you this—there are many on Bourbon Street who don't think that anymore.

I remember one nightclub owner on Bourbon Street early in my ministry. I will call him John. I went in his club one night, but he wouldn't let me talk with him. He tried to run me out, but I ordered a Coke and paid for it. He had to let me stay. I would try to talk with him, but he would walk away.

Night after night I came to his club and ordered a Coke. Some of the girls, who didn't know who I was, started coming to the table to get me to buy them a drink. I would order a Coke, pull out my New Testament and start telling them about Jesus. One night, two of his strippers got saved and walked out. The nightclub owner called the police and tried to get me thrown out. They said that unless I was disturbing the peace, I had just as much right to stay as anyone.

Finally, one night, after a number of his girls had left, the nightclub owner came over to my table, sat down and asked me a question. He looked at me with a scowl on his face and said, "Why do you keep coming here?" Without hesitation I responded, "Because Jesus sent me to you." That man is on his way to heaven today. And it isn't because I did anything so unusual. I simply did the one thing God called Christians to do—tell others the story of Jesus.

Evangelism Was First with Jesus

We are all familiar with the Great Commission that Jesus left us, "Go ye into all the world . . . and preach the gospel." Sometimes we forget that Jesus not only said that, but did it!

Jesus Christ had a three year public ministry where he only did one thing. He spent his entire time trying to get people to transfer their membership from hell to heaven.

The reason why people stopped following Jesus is because evangelism was all he did and it got more dangerous every day.

Whenever Jesus Christ preached, he could get 5,000 people to listen to him as long as he fed them! When Jesus cut the food and simply preached, only 500 showed up.

One day Jesus said, "I'm not going to preach; all I want you to do is come together and pray." Only 120 people showed up.

One day Jesus tried to recruit people who wouldn't hear a sermon but would simply go out in pairs and knock on doors. Only seventy showed up.

And one day Jesus put an ad in the local paper trying to recruit men who would let evangelism be a full-time job. Only twelve responded to the ad, and even one of those was a reject.

One night Jesus said to the eleven he had left, "Gentlemen,

tonight evangelism is going to get a little touchy. We are going to be witnessing to soldiers who are going to be trying to kill us." Only three of the eleven went with him that night.

Finally, Jesus said to the three, "This time our evangelism is going down a dead-end street. At the other end of it there's going to be a cross." Of the three, only one went with him—John.

Think of it—of the 5,000 who ate, and the 500 who listened, and the 120 who prayed, and the 70 who went, and the 11 who worked, and the 3 who dared, only *one* went with him all the way to the cross. And they ended up calling him John, the Evangelist.

Was Jesus proud of John for making evangelism first? Well, you'll have to ask Jesus that. But I know this: on the cross, Jesus told John to take care of his mother. And John wrote the most important of the four Gospels. And Jesus gave John the vision that we have as the last book of the Bible—the book of Revelation. And furthermore, when all of the others were dead, John, at the age of 100, was still telling the world about Jesus.

And before I close, I must add one word. Evangelism is not only first with God, you and Jesus,—but it is also first with the unsaved man. Because you see, that man already has a reservation in hell today. And he can't change it until somebody tells him about Jesus.

5

The Priority of Prayer

Charles G. Fuller

Text: "And it came to pass, that, as he was praying in a certain place, when he ceased, one of his disciples said unto him, Lord, teach us to pray, as John also taught his disciples" (Luke 11:1).

An advertiser, by the name of Barnard, once said, "One picture is worth a thousand words."

Such a statement applies to few subjects more effectively than it does to prayer.

To rub shoulders with one who knows how to pray will probably prove far more productive than to laden one's library shelves with wordy volumes on the matter. The more I read after the people who obviously write out of a magnificent prayer life, the more I seem to hear them say, in effect, "Get to the matter at hand. Learn to pray from prayer itself!"

Could it be otherwise? If such a wondrous experience could be easily articulated, would it not somehow be less than wondrous? In a sense, to talk and write about prayer after you have handled prayer itself, is like politely listening to someone tell you about a place where you have already been.

In 1941 the nation's outstanding college football player was a running back by the name of Tom Harmon. Today Mr. Harmon is a sportscaster and analyst, but in the early 1940's he was the dazzling number 99 in the blue and gold of the University of Michigan.

In his senior year, Tom Harmon was selected to receive the

coveted Heisman Trophy, given annually to the country's leading collegiate football player. To be sure, much excitement surrounded the occasion on which the trophy was awarded, but, according to Harmon, an equally thrilling moment regarding that trophy came a few years ago in his own home.

Mark Harmon, Tom's son, who was thirteen at the time, asked his father a question at the supper table. It seems he had been reading about an award called the Heisman Trophy. Knowing that his father possessed a wealth of sports information, Mark asked his dad, "What is a Heisman Trophy?"

The elder Harmon responded, "Son, I guess the best way to tell you about a Heisman trophy is to *show* you one." So, father and son went into another room where there were a number of trophies and awards which belonged to the former college great. Dad Harmon reached for a particular one and, holding it out for his son to see, said, "Son, this is a Heisman Trophy."

Similarly, to *handle* the trophies of prayer is worth a thousand words on the subject!

Little wonder the disciples of our Lord wanted him to teach them to pray. They had *seen* him pray. They had *heard* him pray. They had *felt* the power of prayer when he talked with the heavenly Father.

So, on a day, during Jesus' earthly ministry, one of the disciples registered a request for himself and the others. He said, "Lord, teach *us* to pray."

Mind you, these men who asked the Lord to teach them to pray were not pagans of some sort. They were, by no means, unacquainted with the subject of prayer. They were "homegrown" Jews, and were instructed in the ways of the nation of God. By Jewish tradition they would pray three times a day. They were aware of what the Old Testament had to say concerning barriers to prayer, such as pride, idolatry, and disobedience. In spite of this knowledge of prayer, they still asked, "Lord, teach us to pray."

Where lies the key to their request? It is to be found in the words just preceding their request.

The Priority of Prayer

Give close attention to Luke's account of the moment as found in verse one of his eleventh chapter: "And it came to pass, that, *as he was praying* in a certain place, when he ceased, one of his disciples said unto him, Lord teach us to pray."

When the disciples heard Jesus pray, they sensed a frailty in their own prayer life. When they asked him for some instruction in prayer, they were not asking for more of what they already knew. They realized he would not respond to them with something tepid or bland. Having caught sight of Jesus at prayer had spoken volumes of inspiration to the disciples. They wanted to be able to pray like he did!

Undoubtedly, this too is the desire of many modern-day Christians. It is not presumptuous, then, to believe that there is a real sense of identity which disciples now have with the disciples who *first* asked, "Lord, teach us to pray."

All too many attempts to learn prayer today, however, seem to run amuck at the level of defining and analyzing prayer. Much of the advice we receive concerning prayer stirs our initial interest but eventually proves to be disappointing because it falls short of what we really wanted to know.

Several years ago my wife received a birthday card which illustrated the difference between a kind of advice we need and the advice we so often get. The card bore an arresting message on its cover. It presumed to tell, "How to Live to Be a Hundred." The inside of the card contained this magnificent bit of innocuity, "Get to be ninety-nine and be very, very careful!"

We need to step off the treadmills of unpromising discussion about prayer and onto the escalator of experiencing prayer itself. After all, how many ways can you define and analyze a child's conversation with his father?

I do not mean to subtract from any of the loftiness of prayer by way of oversimplification, but is not prayer the conversation of a child of God with his heavenly Father? Quite obviously then, the vitality of prayer is in direct proportion to the vitality of the relationship between that child of God and his heavenly Father.

It would appear that our greatest profit in learning the lessons of prayer would be upon the most basic subject matter in its regard.

Perhaps this little incident which took place in our home will drive home the point: Our two younger sons, ages eight and eleven, were having lunch at the kitchen table one Saturday noon. Each bowed his head to offer an inaudible blessing. The eleven-year-old was first to complete his prayer and sat waiting for his younger brother to finish his. The seconds ticked by until it seemed to David, the older boy, that Mike, the younger, was taking more than enough time for a simple blessing. Finally Mike looked up and David asked him, "Have you been praying all that time?"

"Yes," Mike answered, "I was almost finished but I 'muffed it up' and had to start all over again."

Perhaps we would do well to go back to some prayer-beginnings ourselves. There are four rudimental lessons on prayer which need to be learned, or relearned by any Christian who is asking, "Lord, teach us to pray."

Prayer's Reality

The first lesson is that of *prayer's reality*.

From the Christian's standpoint, the reality of prayer is that we *must* pray. It is not only that we *want* to pray, or that we have opportunity to pray. It is that we must pray.

Why is prayer so necessary? Because a child of God who does not pray has a relationship to his heavenly Father which is as peculiar and distant as the relationship of a loving, earthly father to an indifferent child who refuses even to speak to his father.

Just as it is normal for earthly relationships to prompt the desire to communicate, it is only normal, thus a necessity, for a Christian to want to talk with the Lover of his soul.

Furthermore, prayer must be spontaneous and continuous if it is real. To be sure, there are moments for planned, structured conversations between persons who are closely related, but their relationship would be strange indeed if such was the only type of communication they shared. So it is with prayer. There are those daily occasions for planned conversation with God, but if we are silent in his presence otherwise, there is bound to be some question about how intimate we are with him.

Prayer is that means whereby we may be good stewards of God's presence. When questioned about God's omnipresence, we Christians are quick to state our conviction that God is ever, and in all places, present. Have you noticed, however, some approaches to prayer would indicate that God is more distant than near, more to be sought than to be acknowledged?

Have you considered the refreshment which can be yours each morning as you have a conversation with God while driving to the office? Such an experience will underscore the reality of God's presence in your workaday world as well as bedtime devotions punctuate his presence in your home.

Have you capitalized upon "sink-side" prayer while you washed the breakfast dishes? That kind of relaxed conversation with God will deepen the reality of his presence in your Monday-through-Saturday world as well as Sunday worship accentuates his presence in your church.

Prayer is first and foremost the normal means through which a Christian discusses life with God, thus to acknowledge the reality of a relationship and a Presence.

I think at this point we need to be quite honest about our motives for prayer. Are we articulating a relationship or are we primarily interested in the effects and benefits which may result from prayer?

If our primary interest, consciously or unconsciously, is in the effects of prayer we may be involved in little more than a kind of psychedelic devotionalism which majors on side effects. In such cases it is the feeling which is sought, not God's companionship.

If it is the *feeling* of piety, or propriety, or excitement for which prayer is being used, then that is precisely what is taking place, prayer is being *used*.

A minister's ears need to be especially attentive at this point.

If congregations could follow pastors from their pulpits to their prayer closets, would the journey be a disappointing one, interrupted by detours and wrong turns?

One of my vivid memories of a homiletics class during seminary days is that of an evaluation session following one of the student's practice sermons. Each of us in the class was required to preach at various times during the semester and, following that pulpit attempt, the other students were called upon to register criticisms regarding the sermon. After one of the students had finished his sermon, the professor called upon one man in the class to give his reactions. The student pondered a moment and answered, "Sir, it seemed to me that our brother's sermon had a sledgehammer introduction and a tack hammer development."

Could that be descriptive of all too many a minister's prayer practices: sledgehammer pulpiteering linked to a tack hammer prayer life?

For ministers and laymen alike, the first lesson to be learned about prayer is that the vitality of our relationship to God is reflected in the reality of our prayer life.

Prayer's Priority

The second lesson to be learned, or relearned, regarding prayer is the lesson of *prayer's priority*.

In the twenty-fourth chapter of Luke's Gospel we find the Lord further instructing some of those who had earlier asked, "Lord, teach us to pray": "And, behold, I send the promise of my Father upon you: but tarry ye in the city of Jerusalem, until ye be endued with power from on high" (Luke 24:49).

Obedient to our Lord's command regarding prayer, the early believers gathered in an upper room for ten days of praying. Then Luke, in the Acts, records this outcome: "And when the day of Pentecost was fully come, they were all with one accord in one place" (Acts 2:).

Only the slightest reminder is needed for us to recall what happened when that "day of Pentecost was fully come." Upon

The Priority of Prayer 51

hearing Peter's powerful message on the resurrection of Jesus, about 3,000 people committed their lives to Christ.

Practically every phrase-turning preacher has, at one time or another, made sermonic play on these Pentecostal circumstances. He has said something like this: "The early disciples prayed ten days, preached one, and 3,000 souls were converted. We modern Christians pray one day, preach for ten and then wonder why there are not greater results."

There is more involved here, however, than just phraseology and a word-turning cliché. There is perhaps a disturbing revelation here about the lacking priority given to prayer today as a channel of God's power to his people.

I frankly fear what I call "self-help evangelism," which adopts the hackneyed philosophy, "God helps those who help themselves." To be certain, there are times wherein we need God's help, but there are those times when our ability is not adequate for the occasion, thus help alone would be no help. In those moments, we need the mighty power of God's Holy Spirit to do what no man can do!

Have you taken stock of so many of our approaches to evangelism, for instance? We turn the program cranks and pull the promotional levers. We mimeograph and mechanize our way toward a week on the church calendar. Then, in an effort at spiritual propriety, we set up a crash program of prayer like a week of prerevival cottage prayer meetings.

No one would dare suggest that such prayer programs be eliminated, but the situation somewhat reminds me of an incident on the football practice field during my college days.

We had a defensive guard on our squad who was overweight and out of condition. The coaching staff was desperately trying to correct both problems by running this player every chance they could. One afternoon, during a scrimmage session, the player missed an assignment, therefore missed a tackle he should have made. The line coach shouted to him, "Start running the track, son!"

Out onto the quarter-mile track the lad lumbered, lugging his

245 pounds with him. Having finished one lap, he looked at the coach with a plea in his eyes for "mercy," but the coach barked, "Keep running!" After the overweight guard finished the second lap he was panting and hoping upon hope he could stop. But the coach called out, "Keep on running, son. I'm going to run 45 pounds off of you!"

As the player glanced back he plaintively chuckled, "But, coach, you aren't going to do it all in one day, are you?"

Is this illustrative? Do we sometimes try to run off our accumulated repentance, all our overdue reconciliations and our flabby earthiness in a "crash program" of last minute prayer?

Belated revival is only a symptom. The germ is an unlearned lesson. It is the unlearned lesson of prayer's priority.

God has established it. It is his approach to the empowering and equipping of his people. We cannot bypass it. The power of God belongs to those whose prayer life is a forethought, not an afterthought!

Prayer's Practicality

There is still another basic lesson of prayer to be learned or relearned. It is the lesson of *prayer's practicality*.

We give all too little heed to the Bible's resource material on such matters as church administration and congregational psychology. There is a wealth of information, for instance, to be found in the brief second phrase of Acts 2:1: "They were all with one accord in one place."

Prayer had *gathered* those early Christians and prayer had been the experience which *united* them.

Is it not true that there are churches today who would do well to turn to the *pragmatism* of prayer as a uniting force in their midst?

If it is expedient for a church to seek stewardship pledges to underwrite its financial ministry, it is no less practical for a church to regularly confront itself with the stewardship of *prayer investments* in its ministry.

By what means can any group of Christians deeply relate to one another unless they pray for each other?

How can a Christian cope with the unanswerable conflicts of life if he does not find it normal to talk over such matters with an all-wise heavenly Father?

How shall Christians resolve differences if there is no precious fellowship of prayer to share following an apology?

Woven into the very pattern of life for the Christian is God's prayer design. Consequently, to settle for a weak prayer life is to choose a life of spiritual impracticality!

Prayer's Authority

There is still one more lesson of prayer to be learned, or relearned. That fourth lesson is the one regarding *prayer's authority*.

A simple statement of the lesson of prayer's authority is this: A prayerful Christian is in a position to be phenomenally used. Reversely, a prayerless Christian is left too often to the untrustworthiness of his own decisions and devices.

Jesus said that all authority (meaning power over power), is his in heaven and earth. Thus, because he resides in the Christian in the person of the Holy Spirit, that same power can be expressed through us.

However, the Christian who fails to be aware of the presence of Christ within him can hardly be an instrument of that Presence. Prayer is that natural outgrowth of one's awareness of the Lord's nearness. Hence, prayer and the indwelling potential of the Spirit in a Christian are inseparably related.

Indeed, a Christian who is in close and consistent touch with the potent Christ is a Christian who lives with a sense of fresh authority, purpose, and direction.

Several years ago I was preaching for a week in a church in the Washington, D.C., area. Following one of the services I was approached by a young man who identified himself as an executive assistant to one of our United States senators. After exchanging a few pleasantries the young man invited me to take a tour of the Senate office building and to have lunch in the Senate dining room the following day.

The next day, the pastor, the guest musician for the week, the senatorial assistant and I formed a small entourage. After the tour and lunch we were to take in a few more of the interesting sights close at hand. I became rather excited about it all and began walking a few steps ahead of the others in our group.

Seeing a rather interesting looking room I proceeded to walk through the door, only to be suddenly confronted by a sizable Capitol security guard. I recognize authority when I see it, so I timidly halted in my tracks.

Momentarily the other three men in our group came along, and the moment the guard recognized the young executive assistant, he stepped aside. When the guard stepped aside, I quickly joined cadence with my executive friend and smugly entered the room.

After we had gotten into the room, a thought suddenly struck me. I had entered the place not upon my credentials but upon someone else's authority. Someone else's authority had gotten me much farther than I ever could have gone on my own.

Then another thought struck me. This is an illustration of what the power of Christ can do. In his authority we can do what we *never* could do by our own dent of effort!

Is that not what our Lord was saying when he said: "But ye shall receive power, after that the Holy Ghost is come upon you: and ye shall be witnesses unto me both in Jerusalem, and in all Judea, and in Samaria, and unto the uttermost part of the earth" (Acts 1:8).

The disciples of another day said, "Lord, teach us to pray." The disciples of our day make the same request, thus to receive our lesson assignments. Having learned the lessons of prayer's reality, prayer's priority, prayer's practicality, and prayer's authority we can say, "Thank you, Lord, for teaching *us* to pray."

6

In the Interest of Time

William L. Self

Text: Ephesians 5:16.

We stood in the old city of Bern, Switzerland, waiting for the famed old clock to strike the hour. This masterpiece of machinery, dating back to medieval times, had a golden figure coming with a hammer to strike the bell upon the hour. The intricate devices on the face of the clock mark the passing of the hours, phases of the moon, and the eclipses of the moon.

During the tourist season as the clock approaches the hour, a small band of tourists usually gathers at the base of the tower to see the event when the hour is struck and the figures come out from the tower to perform their mechanical task. As we watched, there were families with little children and there were old men and women as well as an abundance of those in their middle years to see the golden man with his hammer strike the bell as he had done for countless centuries.

Just as we could not stop the movement of the hands and the march of the figures around the bell, neither could we stop the movement of time. No prayer, no entreating, no skilled physician can hold it back.

The cancelled stubs of a check book are a good measure of where one's financial priorities have been and where the interests of his own life may be invested. Jesus has said that where a man's treasure is, his heart will be there also. It is also true that the pages of a calendar are a good indication of one's investment of minutes and hours and the substance of which his life is made. Each one of us may have twenty-four hours a day, but where the treasure of these twenty-four hours is invested is an indication of where our hearts may be.

It is common to hear "I don't have time" in a busy, frazzled, hectic world from a person who may be filled with little things to do. However, not having enough hours or minutes is only one dimension of time. To properly understand what time is all about, we must see it as a precious jewel with four sides, each side being part of the whole and yet giving us a different insight into the nature of the whole. We must hold time in our hands and examine it, looking at each of its four sides to properly understand it. First, we must see:

Time as Substance

The ancient Greek said that time could be viewed as being fundamentally circular. For him it had the possibility of repeating itself with events coming around again and again. In his experience time was chronological, something to be measured by a clock or a calendar.

To contrast with this, the Hebrew understood time as being linear, moving as a river with a source, substance, and direction. Though the river moves through rapids and waterfalls, it still moves with a plan and in a direction. The Hebrew was more comfortable with time as a season such as "the time of temptation" or "the day of the Lord" than with time as chronology.

Both understandings of time are preserved in our thinking in the twentieth century, with the emphasis heavily weighted on the chronological. Twentieth-century man struggles primarily against the movement of time, against the hands of the clock moving from hour to hour. He is possessed with the notion that he must stop the clock. He has invested a considerable amount of his ability in this endeavor.

His ability to mask the passing of time is endless. He may use cosmetics or fashions, pills or plaster, paint or varnish. All of these are a part of his arsenal to stop the march of time.

However, biblical man, realizing the impossibility of stopping the march of time, is more concerned with the substance of time than the cessation of its march. Because he experiences time as moving to a point in history with God, the creator, the controller of all events, he knows that nothing happens that God does not allow. Everything happens on God's time. History, according to Biblical man, is made up of "times" in God's hands (Ps. 31:15).

Time as Opportunity

As we turn to examine the next side of the jewel, we come to see that the Bible presents time as opportunity and human response. There are times of natural events such as harvest, marriage, death, and birth. However, these times are of no avail if man does not see the opportunity in each of them. It is of no use for the farmer to try to reap a harvest in sowing time. He must wait for it to be ripe and then gather it in. There is a clear indication in that beautiful passage in Ecclesiastes when the writer says:

"To every thing there is a season, and a time to every purpose under the heaven: a time to be born, and a time to die; a time to plant, and a time to pluck up that which is planted; a time to kill, and a time to heal; a time to break down, and a time to build up; a time to weep, and a time to laugh; a time to mourn, and a time to dance; a time to cast away stones, and a time to gather stones together; a time to get, and a time to lose; a time to keep, and a time to cast away; a time to rend, and a time to sew; a time to keep silence, and a time to speak; a time to love, and a time to hate; a time of war, and a time of peace" (Eccl. 3:1–8).

The location of events that occur in time derive their meaning from two factors, the opportunity that presents itself to man and man's response to the opportunity with appropriate action. Even more important than this is the understanding that it is the creator God who provides the opportunity.

Proper stewardship of time includes the ability to grasp the opportunity that God has provided. It is out of this background that Paul can speak confidently in Ephesians 5:16 of "redeeming the time" or, as the Revised Standard says, "making the most of the time." It is seizing the opportunity in the time.

With this understanding of time as seized opportunity, we have a clearer view of what our salvation is all about. God has provided the opportunity in time for men to come to Christ, for the time of Jesus is seen as a time of opportunity, and to seize this opportunity means salvation. To neglect it is disaster. Because the Jews did not seize the opportunity and rejected Christ, they courted disaster. The Christian, discerning the times correctly, is an heir of salvation. God has provided the time to come to Christ, to grow in grace, to witness to the faith, and to properly use the goods at his disposal. Lowell said it:

> Once to every man and nation comes the moment to decide
> In the strife of truth with falsehood, for the good or evil side;
> Some great cause, God's new Messiah, offering each the bloom or blight,
> And the choice goes by forever 'twixt that darkness and the light.

Shakespeare had a biblical understanding of time. He said:

> There is a tide in the affairs of men,
> Which, taken at the flood, leads on to fortune;
> Omitted, all the voyage of their lives
> Is bound in shallows and in mysteries.

The tragedy of unseized opportunity was reflected by John Oxenham when he said:

> To every man there openeth a way, and ways, and a way
> The high soul treads the high way,
> The low soul gropes the low,
> And in between on the misty flats,
> The rest drift to and fro.

For the sensitive Christian the task becomes even more difficult because he must understand that opportunities sometimes come "in the mask of darkness."

Nothing could have been more distressing than the tyranny of Cromwell and the long Parliament to those who loved the old church and its ways of worship. Stained glass was broken, altars were torn down, and the conduct and participation of the worship of the Church of England rendered one a criminal. In the midst of these years a layman, Sir Robert Shirley, did extraordinary things: he built a church, one very well suited to the worship which had been forbidden and one which still stands in Leicestershire. For his pains, he was summoned by Cromwell to London, confined in a tower, and died. A full discussion of the issues involved in this circumstance is not necessary here, but the inscription placed over the entrance to this old church will help us to understand what it means to seize the opportunity:

"In the year 1653 when all things sacred were throughout the nation either demolished or profaned, Sir Robert Shirley, baronet, founded this church whose singular praise it is to have done the best things in the worst times and hoped them in the most calamitous."

Time is opportunity. But this still does not complete our understanding of time. We must turn it even further and see:

Time as Judgment

If in the Bible we see time as promise and fulfilment, opportunity and response, it is only natural that the manner of the response is to come under the judgment of God.

This concept is introduced to us first of all by Amos when he talks about "the day of the Lord" as a concept of judgment. It is Amos saying that in God's appearing he will come in righteousness and therefore judgment (Amos 5:18–20). From this point on the prophets were concerned that God would judge men on the basis of the use of their opportunities. On "that day" or "the day of the Lord" God would hold man accountable for his stewardship of the opportunities that he had been given.

This is also carried over into the New Testament. We see clearly in the parables of Jesus and specifically in the parable of the talents that we are to be judged on the use and the investment of our opportunities.

When Daniel Webster was asked to relate to a group the most profound thought he ever had, he replied quite simply: "The most profound thought that I have ever had has been my accountability to God." Each of us has been given opportunity. By his grace we have the ability to discern the opportunity in the events of our days. Time by its very nature works its judgment upon us. Perhaps this is what Jesus was talking about in the story of the Last Judgment found in the twenty-fifth chapter of Matthew when men cried out to the Judge: "When saw we thee hungry or athirst and naked?" The reply was: "Inasmuch as ye have done it unto the least of these, ye have done it unto me." The ability to see the opportunity in each moment of the day and to seize it is important for the Christian's use of his time. The final understanding of time is for :

Time as Eternity

It is important for us to understand that a proper Christian understanding of time must see time, which is temporal, being followed immediately by time which is eternal. The peculiarity of man's situation now is that he may at any point of this world's time step into the world to come. In the Fourth Gospel's phrase eternal life is in present possession. This is made clear in Paul's phrase about the ends of the ages having come upon Christians (Eph. 2:6), his conception of the "earnest" of our inheritance which we have here and now. And it is established in Christ's teaching about the new kingdom which has appeared among men with his coming. For the person who lives in the light of the New Testament can see that the time we now have is a filled time. It is Christ-filled. He has a taste of the eternal now. New Testament writers make it crystal clear to us that the foundation of the purpose of God in time has been active through all history and that the coming of Christ was the fulfilment of "the time."

It is imperative in the Christ-filled duration to understand that eternal life is now and that the kingdom is made more real and vivid by the seizing of the opportunities which present themselves and that we have the strength of the eternal as the temporal, chronological days have been turned into the eternal life made available to us in the Christ.

7

Witness Is for Now

Charles L. McKay

Text: "And ye are witnesses of these things" (Luke 24:48).

Some churches grow and reach people with grand success while others bear no fruit. It is the God-given task of a New Testament church to reach people. In areas where there are people, churches can and should reach them. Under similar circumstances, in populated cities, one church reaches additional people, another does not. There must be a reason. Pastors desiring to reach people should find the secret.

God's work in this world is evangelism. By his permissive will in the use of human frailties, the work goes slow at times, but God's eternal purpose and plan cannot be stopped.

From the first announcement of the evangel or gospel in Genesis 3:15 to the great and blessed "whosoever will" of the book of Revelation, God used angels, rulers, prophets, patriarchs, apostles, teachers, preachers, writers, notorious sinners saved by grace, and Jesus Christ himself to share the "good news" to lost men everywhere. And even until now, wherever and whenever the gospel has been faithfully proclaimed, people have embraced Jesus as their Lord and Savior and he has changed their lives. And yet, if it had not been of God and in his power and control, evangelism would have perished long ago at the hands of unfaithful and unworthy stewards.

Evangelism Is a Divine Provision

Salvation in Jesus Christ originated in the heart of God. Redemption is God's move downward to man and not man's

Witness Is for Now 63

upward reach to, or his search for, God. Thus evangelism is of divine origin; it began with God. The first evangelistic promise recorded in the Bible is, "The seed of the woman . . . shall bruise thy head and thou shalt bruise his heel" (Gen. 3:15).

This Scripture sets forth the fact of two direct, opposing forces in the world. These two antagonistic forces are God and the devil. Each seeks to be the master of man. All men apart from Jesus Christ are servants of Satan. They must voluntarily change masters or remain servants to their father the devil. Man, by his own free will had chosen Satan as his master. To be saved from the wrath brought on because of his sin, man must change masters. Redemption is necessary. God offers it through the evangel.

God gave his Son to die for the sins of the world. This good news is the gospel of redemption. Though all men have sinned, therefore being lost and estranged from God, Jesus Christ died to save them. Men must repent for sin and accept Jesus as their Lord and Savior. This good news is offered to everyone, but each one must accept it or else die in his sins.

Ownership by creation was not sufficient if man is to have freedom to choose for himself. Therefore, God made redemption possible. God set out to redeem a family of volunteers. His offer still holds. Wherever and whenever the gospel is preached, some turn their back on Satan and choose Christ as their Lord and Master.

In keeping with his promise in Genesis 3:15, by means of death, Jesus Christ became the mediator between a righteous God and guilty sinners (Heb. 9:15-17). The penalty for sin is death. Since all have sinned, death passed upon all. Unless someone righteous died for all, all must die. Only God was righteous; and God couldn't die. But God in the person of his Son, who became man, could and did die for sin. While in the flesh Jesus restored life to several, but people kept dying. To destroy death, Jesus must get to the source—the devil. Jesus submitted to death, himself. He let it kill him. He died. But the writer to the Hebrews explained: "That through death he might destroy him that had power over death, that is the devil" (Heb. 2:14). By his death and resurrection, Jesus Christ abolished death (2 Tim. 1:10), and he brought life and immortality to light through the gospel.

The story is told of a country boy who made a toy boat which became very dear to him. He spent his spare time playing with his boat in the brook in front of his home. Day by day, with a rope tied to one end, he would throw the boat out into the water and pull it unto himself. It was a pleasure for the little boy to watch the boat plow its way through the water. One day he threw too hard and the rope slipped from his hand and his boat was gone. The current took it away.

Several weeks later, the boy went to town with his father. While his dad was busy here and there, the boy was looking the town over. In the window of the pawn shop, he saw a boat which looked very much like his own. Sure enough, it was his boat. He recognized it immediately. He said to the owner of the store, "Mister, this is my boat; I made it." The man said, "Son, I have money invested in it; in fact, I have fifty cents in that boat. You may have it for fifty cents."

The little fellow ran to find his dad. If only he could buy his boat back! He got the fifty cents and rushed back to get his boat. After he had redeemed it with the fifty cents, he went down the street, with a tight grip on his boat, saying, "You are mine, little boat, you are mine. You're mine first, because I made you and again you're mine because I bought you."

Our heavenly Father can say to those of us who are redeemed, "You are mine because I made you and you are mine because I redeemed you." Not with corruptible things such as silver and gold but with the precious blood of Jesus Christ he bought us. We belong to God.

Christians Are Stewards of Evangelism

The same homeless Galilean who said, "The foxes have holes and birds have nests but the Son of man hath no place to lay his head," is the One who delivered the divine mandate known by his followers as the Great Commission. On the resurrection side of the grave, our Lord spake saying, "All power is given unto me in heaven and in earth. Go ye therefore, and teach all nations, baptizing them in the name of the Father, and the Son, and of the Holy Ghost: Teaching them to observe all things whatsoever I have commanded you: and, lo, I am with you alway, even unto the end of the world" (Matt. 28:18–20). Add to this Great Commission the words, "Ye are witnesses of these things" (Luke 24:48).

If someone asks, "What things" let Jesus answer: "And he said unto them, Thus it is written and thus it behooved Christ to suffer and to rise from the dead the third day, and that repentance and remission for sins should be preached in his name among all nations, beginning in Jerusalem." Therefore, every Christian is a witness.

Ownership of everything fixed in God, demands stewardship of man. The Apostle Paul asked, "What hast thou that thou didst not receive?" (1 Cor. 4:7). Everything we possess, we have received. For the Bible says, "We brought nothing into this world, and it is certain we can carry nothing out" (2 Tim. 6:7). Shrouds don't have pockets. How many armored cars have you ever seen following a funeral procession? Therefore, the wise thing to do is to "lay up treasure in heaven where neither moth nor rust doth corrupt and where thieves cannot break through and steal." Heavenly treasures must be sent on up ahead. God permits us to lay up for ourselves treasures in heaven. But there is more to Christian stewardship than money. Every Christian is a steward of the gospel commissioned by Jesus himself, who said, "As my Father hath sent me, even so send I you."

Ready to go back to the Father, having finished his work here on this earth, the Son of God left the disciples with this message: "Ye are witnesses of these things." The Scripture further says, "Let the redeemed of the Lord say so." They are to tell it. If you know Christ in the forgiveness of sin, you are to tell it. If you have a Savior who saved you, then you ought to tell other lost people about this Savior who is able to save them. The Great Commission involves every Christian. Preachers are stewards of the gospel. No one is more responsible to be a witness than is a preacher. He is an evangelist in possession of the evangel with a divine mandate to proclaim it. If he is faithful to this stewardship, the power of the Holy Spirit will validate his witness. To this stewardship I am committed.

Mothers and fathers are responsible to God to march under the marching orders of Christ. Having accepted Jesus Christ as Savior, daddy and mother have the responsibility to do their best to lead all the children into the ark of God, the ark of safety—the family of God. Take Noah, for example; he had so lived before, and witnessed to his family, that when the ark was finished and God said, "Come in," his whole family went in with him. It is a reproach to fathers or mothers who have boys and girls who have no confidence in their Christianity.

I have never known many children who were brought up by Christian mothers and fathers who set the right example, who have not come to know Christ in the forgiveness of sin. Parents should go after their children for Jesus. The first place for a Christian father or mother to put his or her foot forward for Christ is in the home. Mr. Burbank said on one occasion that if he didn't give any more attention and any more time to the cultivation of his plants than many mothers and fathers do to the rearing of their children, he would have a garden of weeds. Most juvenile delinquency is due to delinquency of parents.

Let me tell you about two homes. The mother, with her little girl, was visiting an art gallery. They were looking at the portraits of different people on the wall. Presently they came to one, different from all the rest. The little girl was attracted to a picture of Jesus and she said, "Mother, who is that?" The mother replied, "That's Jesus." Then the little girl said, "Mother, who is Jesus?" The mother answered, "Jesus was a man; come along honey." And away she went.

May God have mercy upon any mother who doesn't know enough about Jesus, when the opportunity presents itself, to win her child to Christ. May the Lord pity any child in such a home! It was Jesus who took little children into his arms and said, "Of such is the kingdom of God."

The other was a very poor home. The walls were smoked from lamps without chimneys. On the wall of this home was a faded picture of Jesus as he stood with his head bowed and his hands tied before Pilate. One day the little girl in that home was attracted in a peculiar way to that picture. She called to her mother and said, "Mother, I want you to tell me again about this picture." The busy mother dropped her work and went to a chair where she could sit with the little girl in her arms and looked up at the picture. That morning she pointed that child, who was seeking the way of truth and light, to the Lamb of God who taketh away the sin of the world. This is what Jesus expects from parents.

You remember the story of David who climbed a stairway one day crying, "O Absalom, my son Absalom, would to God that I had died for you." If David had realized his responsibility toward the children in his home and had lived for them, I believe we would have a different story in the Bible. One wants to ask David, why didn't you live for your boys? Why didn't you set the right kind of example before them?"

Parents today should profit by David's mistake. Evidently David made a good king, but he is a very poor example of a good parent. A seminary professor's son said, "My daddy spent his time writing books and serving other people. He made a good leader for others, but he never got acquainted with his family. He was a poor daddy."

Teachers, too, are stewards of the gospel. Every Sunday School teacher and officer is a steward of the manifold grace of God and ought to witness to this grace. For six or seven years before I was called to the ministry, I was superintendent of a Sunday School. I remember going to Jackson, Mississippi, to a state Sunday School convention.

Dr. P. E. Burroughs, from the Sunday School Board in Nashville, brought the main message that day. I shall never forget a story that he told. He told us about a First Baptist Church in a great city. The pastor didn't seem to be concerned for the poor people in the slum sections of the city, nor did the Sunday

School superintendent and teachers. But, he said that there was one teacher, whom he called "Miss Mary" who did care. So she went down into one such area and with her own money she rented a vacant house. She went out into the streets daily and gathered in the neglected boys who were roving the streets.

Upstairs in that upper room, Miss Mary would open the Bible and tell these boys the story of God's love, and how Christ died for their sins. One by one they came to know Christ as their personal Savior.

One day, two of her boys were catching a ride on a train as it switched in and out of the yard. One of them slipped between the wheels and his body was bruised and crushed—crushed unto death—but he lived a little while. The other boy, his companion, who was with him, and others who had gathered around heard the dying boy whispering, "Miss Mary, Miss Mary." Charlie's friend said, "Charlie is calling for his Sunday School teacher."

Miss Mary was summoned. When she arrived, she sat on the end of a cross tie and pulled Charlie's broken and torn body up into her lap. As she sat holding him, he whispered, "Miss Mary, will Jesus be hard on me now?" Miss Mary said, "No, Charlie, Jesus loves you, son. He died for you. He saved you. You have trusted Him. He won't be hard on you, Charlie." Dr. Burroughs said that this good Sunday School teacher said, "Little Charlie smiled and in a moment his little spirit slipped out of my arms into the arms of his Savior."

The pastor failed Charlie. The superintendent failed Charlie. The mother failed her child. The daddy failed his son. But the teacher said, "I can't fail Charlie." Teachers are witnesses and they are under obligation to do so.

In all my years I never had a Sunday School teacher to say a word to me about my soul's salvation or my relation to Jesus Christ as my Savior. My parents took me to Sunday School before I can remember. I grew up attending church and Sunday School. We never missed. What was the matter? Did my teachers know Jesus? Did they want me to know him? Did they really care? Why did they not say so?

Someone may say, "I am not a preacher, and you said that it is the preacher's business to win souls. I am not a mother nor a father, and you say that it is their business to win souls. I am not a teacher, and you said that it is a teacher's responsibility. Do you have a word for me?" Yes, I do. Jesus said, "Ye are witnesses of these things." This, he says to every Christian. Then every Christian is a steward of the gospel.

During a period of twelve years a friend of mine has found, retrieved, and delivered forty-two bodies of people who have drowned in the lakes of Arizona. This is an average of three and one half each year. Without remuneration and at his own expense in equipment, travel, and time, this man has given all of his spare time after working hours, nights, and week-ends searching for these bodies. Three months is the longest time that it has taken to locate a dead body. If Christians spent one third the time searching for lost souls that this man does for lost bodies, there would be many to hear the "well done" of their Lord when he returns.

With the contrast of the difference in value of a lost body and a lost soul made by Jesus, why is it so difficult to get Christians to seek the lost when men will dedicate themselves to projects of so much less value?

One day Jesus put a little spittle and clay upon the eyes of a blind man and healed him. This blind man immediately went out telling people what had happened to him. He had something good to tell, and he went about telling it. The fruit of a Christian is another Christian. If you have never brought another to Jesus, then you are fruitless. Every Christian can win someone to Christ.

Let me tell you about a faithful steward: He was a man who could not speak because he stuttered. He wouldn't dare try to talk to anyone about his soul, because of his defective speech. He couldn't talk, but he had a way to bring people to church and he used what he had. He did what he could. A revival was going on in his church. Night after night he brought lost men to church to hear the gospel preached. During the revival, twenty of them accepted Christ as their Savior. He could not talk to them, but he could bring them to church to hear one, who could talk, tell about Jesus. He always sat in the rear of the church house and prayed for his men while his pastor preached.

The outstanding thing about Andrew is that he brought his brother to Christ immediately after he, himself, had found Jesus. If you know Jesus Christ then you are a witness of these things.

Man is a steward, and it is required in a steward that he be faithful. When Jesus Christ returns to this earth, he will have all his stewards give account of themselves, and they will have to acknowledge whether or not they have been faithful.

After teaching school seven years, God called me to preach. It was necessary to go away to school for special training. We had to leave our beautiful four-hundred-acre farm, along with the cattle and horses, with someone until everything could be sold. A good friend of ours (we thought he was a good friend), said to me, "I will see after your farm." I agreed to let him farm the land one year. For one half the crop, he was to farm the land. When time came to sell the cotton, Jay wrote that it would please him to hold the cotton for a better price. This was agreeable.

To my amazement, when I reached home Christmas, the cotton had been sold and all the money had been spent. We were in partnership; we were both to have shared in the increase, but he took all and gave us none. What was I to do? Let the law take its course? Yes, and it did.

All too many people treat God like that. They have to be tracked down by the Lord for collection. My partner paid off the hard way. Many of us too often do. Privileges impose obligations. Citizenship requires taxes. Rights and benefits come with a price tag. The Bible says, "Render, therefore, unto Caesar the things that are Caesar's; and unto God the things that are God's."

The Scope of Our Stewardship

Paul answered for himself by saying, "As much as in me is" (Rom. 1:15). Jesus said, "But ye shall receive power, after that the Holy Ghost is come upon you: and ye shall be witnesses unto me both in Jerusalem, and in all Judea and in Samaria and unto the uttermost part of the earth" (Acts 1:8).

Soon after I moved to Arizona a friend invited me to go with a group to Utah on a deer hunt. Never having hunted in the West, I had to get equipped for it. When I purchased my deer rifle, the salesman insisted that in this country a scope is a must. So I bought a scope. Neither the salesman, nor my host with whom I was going hunting, told me that a scope must be sighted in. They had no idea that I was so dumb. They thought surely I had that much sense or I shouldn't go hunting.

After we pitched our tent in the middle of the hunting ground, I was so excited that I didn't sleep that first night. Before day dawned, we were all scattered across the territory waiting for the light. By the time it was good day, I saw four big trophies standing in the bed of the creek within forty steps of me. We were to be on the hunt five days but, thought I, in five minutes I'll have my limit. At that time, the limit was three. I pulled the rifle down, scoped the best one, emptied my gun and didn't touch a hair. Those deer looked at me as though to say, "Try it again."

By the time I had refilled the clip with bullets the deer had disappeared into the brush. Having never used a scope before, I decided to try without it. So, I took the scope off of the rifle. Within fifteen minutes I had killed a deer 300 yards away. The fellows had some fun out of a "nut" who didn't know to sight in his scope before using it.

Christians need their missionary or evangelistic scopes sighted in. Jesus said, "But ye shall receive power, after that the Holy Ghost is come upon you, and ye shall be witnesses unto me both in Jerusalem, and in all Judea, and in Samaria, and unto the uttermost part of the earth."

Some people have zeroed their scope in on Jerusalem, but the rest of the world they have not seen. Some zero in on Home Missions, others Foreign Missions. The scope of my stewardship of the gospel is the whole world. Jesus taught that the field is the world. When it comes to the scope of responsibility, all too many miss the meaning of the key word "both" in Acts 1:8. Let me illustrate what I mean.

Tired and hungry, after one o'clock, when he got out of extended session, my five year old grandson came running into the cottage at Glorieta pleading, "Papa, I want, both a jelly sandwich, a peanut butter sandwich, and a bologna sandwich." This five year old taught me what the word "both" means. It means "at the same time." Right now, as soon as possible, at the same time you are to witness in Jerusalem, Judea, Samaria and the uttermost parts of the earth. The world is the scope of stewardship of evangelism for the Christian.

Southern Baptists have the greatest plan known to man whereby a Christian can "at the same time" fulfil his duty to the gospel at home and around the world.

Of course, every blood-bought child of God is responsible to share the gospel, person to person in the community where he lives. A person is a hypocrite who pretends to love lost people overseas and sends money for the same but who will not share his testimony with the neighbors next door, the child in the house, the man in the shop, or the prospect on the job.

While some of us share the gospel at home, God calls others to go as missionary evangelists to other lands. The Bible says, "How shall they believe except they hear and how shall they hear without a preacher and how shall they preach except they be sent?" (Rome. 10:13–15).

While witnesses at home, we can give our tithes and offerings through our church and see that our church sends an equitable share through the Cooperative Program to share the cost of winning the lost around the world.

I have a very dear friend who is a deacon in one of our Southern Baptist churches in Arizona. He has not always belonged to a Southern Baptist Church, but he has been a Baptist for years. How my friend came to join our church is of real interest and a vital point of my message. For lack of a better program his former church decided to send one missionary to one country overseas. A young lady in the church surrendered to be the missionary. She happened to be the niece of my friend. Let me call him Jim. The church sent her as a missionary. Several years they supported her with pride and joy. This church could support only one missionary in one place. They were not going into Judea, Samaria, and the uttermost part of the earth. Yet they were at least sharing the gospel.

Finally, the church changed pastors and the new pastor didn't know the missionary nor was his interest in the particular field where she was serving. Before too many months the church had withdrawn its support. This uncle supported his niece as long as he could. Then, he had to bring her home at his expense.

When Jim first joined one of our churches, he told me why. He had heard about a church and a denomination that had a program where each church, large or small, could share through the Cooperative Program. More than 2,000 missionaries in 70 or more countries overseas are supported in addition to more than 2,000 missionaries in the homeland—all at the same time. Every missionary is guaranteed support and has the assurance of being brought home when time comes. He said, "Only God could provide such a program, and that's the church for me." Jim moved his membership.

The tragedy of sin makes evangelism necessary. The love of God, manifest in Jesus Christ made it available. Faithful stewardship of evangelism by those redeemed by the gospel is God's method of sharing this "good news" with the world.

8

Redeem the Time

Herschel H. Hobbs

Texts: "See then that ye walk circumspectly, not as fools, but as wise, redeeming the time, because the days are evil" (Eph. 5:16).

"Walk in wisdom toward them that are without, redeeming the time" (Col. 4:5).

"What shall I do, Lord?" (Acts 22:10). This was the first question Paul asked after becoming a Christian. Years later, of a life spent in the Lord's service, he said, "I was not disobedient unto the heavenly vision" (Acts 26:19). His Christian life was a demonstration of the proper stewardship of time.

Now as an old man he is in prison in Rome (Philem. 9). He looks back upon a life well-spent. Ahead lies his appearance before Nero. He faces the possibility that his life on earth may soon come to an end. In retrospect, the years since his Damascus road experience seem so short. He is keenly aware of the brevity and uncertainty of life. So short a time, and so much to do!

It is significant, therefore, that in Ephesians and Colossians, both written during his Roman imprisonment, Paul exhorts his readers with the words "redeeming the time." While variously translated, the common idea is to make the most of time and opportunity in life which is so fleeting.

"Redeeming the time." The word rendered "redeeming" was a commercial term. The Greek word for market place is *agora*.

The verb used by Paul is *exagarazō,* to buy out of the market place. So he urges his readers to go into the market place, and buy "the time." "Time" is not *chronos,* or chronological time. It is *kairos,* the opportune time. So the idea is not that of seeking to live a long life, but one with deep meaning. It is to seize the opportune time, to use life and its opportunities in the service of Christ. Two reasons are given for this. Negatively, "because the days are evil" (Eph.). Positively, that their lives may be wisely used as a witness "toward them that are without" or non-Christians (Col.).

Evil powers are at work in every age. And the Lord's people can best oppose them by lives that reveal the power of Christ to change life from waste to witness, from defeat to victory, and from frustration to meaning.

As a Christian you are a steward of life and its opportunities to serve God by serving men. A steward was a housemanager, usually a slave, in charge of his owner's property. He owned nothing, but was responsible for everything. His purpose of being was to benefit his owner, not himself.

Our theme is the stewardship of time. This has to do, not with how long you live, but with how well you live. As all of your money belongs to God, so does all of your life belong to him. And no amount of money given can be in lieu of your life. God seeks you first of all, and then yours. And no person can claim to be a good steward until he has given both. Money is but a part of time, energy, and ability crystallized. And all the money given cannot pay someone else to live for you.

You would do well, therefore, to heed words from Benjamin Franklin. "Dost thou live life? Then do not squander time, for that is the stuff life is made of." And "one today is worth two tomorrows; what I am to be I am now becoming."

Men figure time as past, present, and future. In reality time is all *present.* The *opportune time* is *now!* Yesterday is history. Tomorrow is uncertain. Yesterday is opportunities lost or used. Tomorrow is a will-o'-the-wisp which we never capture.

> Yesterday is only a dream,
> Tomorrow only a vision;
> But today, well lived, makes every yesterday
> A dream of happiness and of every tomorrow
>   A vision of hope.
> Look well, therefore, to this day.

This is an unknown poet's way of saying, "Redeeming the time."

Let me suggest three reasons why as a Christian you should redeem the time.

In the first place, you should redeem the time, because, as Franklin says, what you are to be you are now becoming. The character that you will have, the life that you will be tomorrow, is being forged today. If you delay today, you will delay tomorrow. And before you know it, your life will be over—with nothing worthwhile done. The epitaph on many tombstones might well read:

John Doe
Born——Died

with nothing in between.

Many Christians are good, but good for nothing.

Paul warned against this in 1 Corinthians 3:12–15. A life founded in Christ may be built out of wood, hay, or stubble. In the final test of fire the life's work will be burned up, useless. "If any man's work shall be burned, he shall suffer loss: but he himself shall be saved; yet so as by fire" (v. 15).

While this may apply to any Christian, Paul's example referred specifically to preachers. A pastor can be the busiest or laziest man in town. He punches no clock, and no one follows him to see that he does his job. But One knows. It is he who judges all men. How many preachers will be saved, "yet so as by fire?"

But let no man point the accusing finger at another. He should look to himself. Recently I was working a crossword puzzle. The word to be found was one denoting "a preacher's job." The correct word was "evangelist." "So true, yet so limited in scope. It may have been good puzzle-making, but it was poor theology. For being an evangelist, a bearer of the good news of salvation, is, in the words of Charles Matthews, "Every Christian's Job."

How long has it been since you spoke to a lost person about Christ? Or paused to speak a kind word, do a helpful deed—in his name? If the answer shames you, do not say, "I will do better tomorrow." For tomorrow will never come. Begin today! And you will be more likely to do the same tomorrow, yea, all of the tomorrows.

One of our greatest problems today is the proper use of leisure time. Does it mean for you more time to serve the Lord? Or to do things which will not matter tomorrow if they had not been done?

Boredom is a widespread disease today, because so many seem unable to find something to do to fill their idle moments and days. Long ago Shakespeare said, "If all the years were playing holidays, to sport would be as tedious as to work." It would be far better if we would realize that while each day must be lived unto itself, we are living for eternity in that one day. And each day should be so lived that at bedtime we can sleep the sleep of the weary, made so by toil in the Lord for others, rather than to toss on a sleepless pillow of regret over opportunities wasted.

Goethe says it for us:

> Lose the day loitering. 'Twill be the same story
> Tomorrow, and the next more dilatory.
>
> For indecision brings its own delays,
> And days are lost lamenting over lost days.
>
> Are you in earnest? Seize this very minute!
> What you can do, or think you can, begin it!
> Boldness has genius, power, and magic in it!
>
> Only engage, and when the mind grows heated,
> Begin it, and the work will be completed.

I relate the following incident to introduce a confession. Several years ago Mrs. Hobbs and I were in Mobile, Alabama, for a speaking engagement in a former pastorate. With the pastor and his wife we were entering an eating place. We met two young couples who were leaving. We stopped with the pastor for a brief greeting. As we were introduced to them, one of the men spoke to me.

"I am Bob Norman. When you were pastor of the Calvary Baptist Church in Birmingham, you led me to Christ. One Wednesday afternoon I was at the church for the Junior R.A. meeting. As we met in the hall, you stopped me and asked if I were a Christian. I said, 'No.' You took me in a classroom, explained the plan of salvation, and led me to receive Jesus as my Savior. I have been pastor of the First Baptist Church in Prichard. I am leaving tomorrow to become the pastor of the Belmont Heights Baptist Church in Nashville."

Today he is one of the finest pastors and preachers among us. He is now, and will become increasingly so, one of the young leaders in our denomination. Frankly, I had forgotten the incident. But he remembered. And I thank God now that I was led of the Lord to redeem that opportune moment as a young pastor in his first pastorate since leaving the seminary.

And now the confession. Through the years since then the Lord through the brethren has given me many opportunities to serve. But I cannot help but wonder that while I was busy here and there, how many possible prophets of God have slipped through my fingers because I was too *busy* to redeem other such opportune times.

In the second place, you should redeem the time because opportune times now present will soon be gone. Jesus said, "I must work the works of him that sent me, while it is day: the night cometh, when no man can work" (John 9:4).

Some people live in the past, talking about what they have done. Others live in the future, talking of what they will do. The wise man lives in the present. He never puts off until tomorrow what he should do today. Longfellow once wrote, "Look not mournfully [or proudly] into the past; it returns no more; wisely improve the present, and go forth into the shadowy future without fear and with a manly heart."

The energies of today should not be wasted worrying about tomorrow. Christians should follow the admonition of Jesus in Matthew 6:34. They should not be divided in mind or overly anxious over tomorrow. Tomorrow will have its own cares to be met. "Sufficient unto the day is the evil thereof." In other words, you have enough to do worrying about the duties of today without borrowing trouble from tomorrow. Do your duty today. And it will enable you better to be prepared for the opportunities of tomorrow.

"No man ever sank under the burden of the day. It is when tomorrow's burden is added to the burden of today that the weight is more than a man can bear. Never load yourselves so. If you find yourselves so loaded, at least remember this: it is your own doing, not God's. He begs you to leave the future to Him, and mind the present" (George McDonald).

This is why a wise, merciful God does not unveil to us the future. Without knowing what another day may bring forth, we can concentrate our energies on doing the duties of today. Thomas Carlyle probes our hearts in his words:

> So here hath been dawning
>   Another blue day;
> Think, wilt thou let it
>   Slip uselessly away?

Redeeming today's opportune time is especially important for parents. You have your children under your care and guidance for so short a time. Now you can say, "Do this!" and "Don't do that!" But what about the time when they are no longer with you? In the present you can only, by precept and example, sow seeds of righteousness in their hearts, so that they will become guiding principles for them when they must make life's decisions for themselves. Such opportunities so seized now will bear a rich and gladsome harvest in the future for them, you, and all men. But opportune times which go unredeemed now will bear only heartache in the future.

Years ago in a college pastorate I knew a man who had lived a godless life. And had taught his sons to do the same. For fifty-three years he had not been inside a church. Despite all this, his daughter was a Christian. But when she would tune her small radio to a religious program, her father, to show his contempt for religion, would place it on the floor and kick it about even as the program was coming through it.

Finally, his aged father died. In his grief I was able to talk to him about Christ. He promised to be in Sunday School and church the next day. To the surprise of the church people, he was there. That night he made a profession of his faith in Christ. It was the last time I recall hearing anyone *shout* in church. It was his aged mother who did so.

He plunged into serving the Lord as ardently as he had served the devil. Eventually, he became a deacon in the little church. But one day he came to me brokenhearted. I shall never forget the story that he poured out to me wet with his tears.

"Preacher, you know the kind of man I've been, and the life I've lived. In it all I led my five boys astray. Today I tried to lead one of them to Christ. With bitterness and scorn, he said, 'Dad, you made me what I am. So leave me alone!' Preacher, I could not even lead my own boy to Christ! I know that I am saved, and if I died right now I would go to heaven. But I am living in a saved man's hell!"

The tragedy of not redeeming the opportune time! In the third place, you should redeem the opportune time because it gives you a reason for living. Yes, for Christ to live in you. And you do not really live until you live a life dedicated to him and his work.

To so many people life is meaningless. It is but a fleeting moment between two boundless eternities. For such, life is a drudge, a blank, and they leave behind nothing to show that they have

Redeem the Time

been here. The only mark that they make on the world is to fall down in the mud.

But, thank God, there are others who learn to live. They discern that life has meaning. And they so live as to make it a gladsome thing for themselves, their contemporaries, and for those who come after them.

Such a person was Louise Prichard. She had enough sorrow in her life to break the spirit of anyone made of lesser stuff. But she never wavered nor lost her faith. While wealthy, she was never pretentious. Numbered among her friends were the rich and poor, people in both high and low places. One night in our church we had a guest speaker at a dinner. I told him that perhaps the wealthiest woman in our state was in the room. When asked to pick her out, he failed. Then I pointed to a little lady walking from table to table pouring coffee for the dinner. She was the kind of person who embodied the words of an anonymous writer:

Take time to work—it is the price of success;
Take time to think—it is the source of power;
Take time to play—it is the secret of perpetual youth;
Take time to read—it is the foundation of wisdom;
Take time to worship—it is the highway to reverence;
Take time to be friendly—it is the road to happiness;
Take time to dream—it is hitching our wagon to a star;
Take time to love and be loved—it is the privilege of the gods [of God].

Through time and a series of circumstances of sorrow in her life, Mrs. Hobbs and I came to have an unusually close relationship with her, almost that of mother and children. At one point our church was erecting a new building, including a beautiful chapel. One day I asked her if she would like to give the church the money for this chapel. The amount was a sizeable sum. Without hesitation she agreed. At my request she permitted me to read to the church her commitment, with the hope that it would encourage others to give. The desired result was achieved. When the chapel was finished, without her knowledge we named it after her. Talking with her about a plaque to that effect, she requested that it be small and simple. I suggested that it read:

> THE LOUISE PRICHARD CHAPEL
> a gift of her love to the glory of God

Her only words were "That is perfect!"

However, the story does not end there. It really only begins. For in that gift she discovered how much joy there was in giving money to the Lord. Through the following years she gave fabulous sums through her church to be used as the church willed, but always requesting that a substantial part of each gift should go to missions. She did this without any publicity. One day I received a letter from her containing a large check. When I called to thank her, she said, "Don't thank me. I get more joy out of it than anyone else. I just thank my Lord that he has enabled me to do it."

One Sunday afternoon Mrs. Hobbs and I were visiting her, since she was confined to her bed with a broken hip. I had left the bedroom. It was then that she said to my wife, "Honey, I am rewriting my will. Do you have any suggestions?" Mrs. Hobbs said, "Yes, I do. When during the depression of the 1930's my husband and I were in college, and our own funds were exhausted, we could always get a few dollars from a Ministerial Aid Fund someone had established. Without it, I doubt that we could have made it. I have always hoped to see someone establish a ministerial scholarship fund at Oklahoma Baptist University." Mrs. Prichard simply said, "I like that!"

Now Mrs. Hobbs was thinking in terms of $100,000. But after Mrs. Prichard's death, it was learned that, apart from a few family bequests, she had left her entire estate for this purpose. Its value is in excess of five and one-half million dollars. It is to be used for students preparing for the pastorate and for missionary work.

Mrs. Hobbs had redeemed the opportune time by making a simple suggestion. But Mrs. Prichard in a far greater way redeemed her opportune time by leaving behind a sum which will enable her, through others, to preach the gospel throughout the earth and until Jesus comes again.

At the time of Mrs. Prichard's death her granddaughter and her husband, Mr. and Mrs William Ratliff, Jr., told us that we had increased her lifetime by at least ten years. For we had given her a purpose for living—to do all that she could for others with what the Lord had done for her.

She had caught the spirit of Paul's words, "Redeeming the time, because the days are evil."

9

Love's Labor Lasts

J. D. Grey

Paul, after giving that marvelous, glorious resurrection chapter, carrying us from one great mountain peak to another of a Mount Everest of spiritual nature, says, "Therefore, my beloved brethren, be ye steadfast, unmovable, always abounding in the work of the Lord, forasmuch as ye know that your labour is not in vain in the Lord." (1 Cor. 15:58).

One of Shakespeare's plays was entitled "Love's Labour Lost." It was presented before Queen Elizabeth I in 1598 for the first time. It was more blank verse than rhyme, and is a light love story. Beloved, the title does not need to apply to our labor of love for Christ our Lord because the Christian knows that in this matter it is not a case of "love's labor lost," but that it is a case of "love's labor lasts."

I believe that every worker for Christ in whatever realm he's laboring should take as his motto those lines I saw once on the wall of the study of a preacher friend of mine:

> Just one life, 'twill soon be past,
> Only what's done for Christ will last.

The words of our text say the same thing in another way. "Always abounding in the work of the Lord . . . forasmuch as ye know that your labour is not in vain in the Lord."

Let me point out first of all in this text, the right road to true immortality. Man thinks about immortality. From the earliest recorded history, from time immemorial, man has tried very eaher beloved hills. She was perfect. The professor was elated. He called her to the front of the class and said, "Young ladies and young gentlemen, I want you to realize that what you have just heard is real art!"

The opening night of the play was an unforgettable experience for the entire cast, but especially for the chief character, Mrs. Pearce. The author of the play was present.

At the close of the performance the professor brought the author backstage. He had kind words for all members of the cast. When he came to Mrs. Pearce he took both of her hands in his and, looking deeply into her anxious eyes, said, "My dear, tonight, you put into flesh and blood the woman I dreamed on paper." Mrs. Pearce had simply let a part of her background shine through.

Our lives reflect our background. The same is true when a person has had an experience with Christ. The conversion experience becomes a part of one's background and is reflected in the kind of life which is lived.

It happened to the Apostle Paul when he was transformed during his encounter with Jesus on the road to Damascus. Paul learned in that experience that without God as revealed through Jesus Christ there is no explanation of life. Paul discovered that he could only know the true meaning of life through Jesus Christ, the Son of God.

Out of his background of this discovery that Christ is Lord, Paul wrote these significant words to the church at Corinth: "Therefore, seeing we have this ministry."

Paul recognized that he had received a treasure which must be shared with others. It was "the ministry of the new agreement," as J. B. Phillips translates this phrase. Immediately Paul became responsible for the stewardship of the gospel. There is a parallel to this in our lives.

A glance at Paul's life will illustrate the way his background is reflected in his daily living. As Saul he mirrored his concepts by persecuting the church and those who believed in Jesus Christ. After his conversion he felt the urgency to share his newfound possession with others. He felt the burden and privilege of the stewardship of the gospel.

In parallel experiences, we who have become followers of Christ share the same urgency of the stewardship of the gospel.

The responsibility for the stewardship of the ministry of the new agreement—the stewardship of the gospel—permeates our lives and we become
> undaunted messengers of the gospel,
>> proclaiming an undiluted message,
>>> demonstrating an unselfish ministry,
>>>> and serving an unequalled Master.

Undaunted Messengers

When Jesus established the church he said to Peter, "Upon this rock I will build my church" (Matt. 16:18). By this he meant that upon persons like Peter, James and John—and you and me—he would build his church. He would build his church on persons whose lives had been transformed by his Spirit, and who had faith in Christ. The destructive forces of this world would not defeat his church.

The disciples of Jesus, the Apostle Paul, and others throughout the centuries of time are illustrations of God's continuing incarnation in men. He is building his church through the lives of those persons willing to serve as stewards of the gospel.

The book of Acts records the fact that God used Paul and his witness to expand the church. The New Testament is the record of how the followers of Christ were used to help the church grow. Many have shared in this ministry of the new agreement.

Once I asked my congregation how many had heard a sermon from the twenty-ninth chapter of Acts. Without reflecting for a moment, many in the congregation were tricked into lifting their hands. Of course they were wrong, because Acts has only 28 chapters!

Yet, in another sense of the word they were right, because each generation of Christians is writing the continuing story of God's indwelling in the lives of his followers. We are writing the twenty-ninth chapter of Acts. Each of us is a steward in sharing the gospel.

Go—Tell

Paul is not only an illustration of God's continuing incarnation in men, but as such he was an undaunted messenger. Although he suffered greatly from a difficulty he described as a "thorn in the flesh" (2 Cor. 12:7), still he was undaunted. Even though Paul described his bodily presence as "weak, and his speech contemptible" (2 Cor. 10:10), he refused to become disheartened. His spirit was undaunted. In the face of numerous experiences of suffering in his service for Christ, he did not lose heart.

>He was whipped.
>>He was beaten.
>>>He was stoned.
>>He was shipwrecked.
>>>He was in peril, from robbers, his own people, the heathen, and false brethren.
>>>He was weary, in pain, hungry, thirsty and cold.

In the crucible of these experiences he remembered his conversion, his call and God's great mercy through Christ. He felt worthy of God's wrath, but was given God's mercy through Christ.

However, it was not Paul's nature to linger in the past. He was driven by the urgency of the hour to the task at hand of sharing the good news with everyone. He was an undaunted messenger.

Undiluted Message

Years ago, at the time of my graduation from college, my father, who was a dentist, gave me a graduation gift. It was a study edition of the Bible. On the flyleaf of this book he penned his congratulatory wish for my graduation. He wrote:

May the precious words of this Book inspire
and strengthen you on your journey up the hill of life.
May it add strength and bravery to your weak and weary moments
and cause your character to be higher than your intellect.
May it bring wisdom to your thoughts
and words to your tongue that will bless humanity
in order that the world
may be constantly enriched by the Christ Spirit.

The words my dad wrote reflect the deep confidence he had in the message of the Bible. He believed that if I would study the Word of God, I would be helped by it and, as a result, be a help to others. The Apostle Paul faced many serious charges. He denied that he had misused the Scriptures. He said, "We use no hocus-pocus, no clever tricks, no dishonest manipulation of the Word of God. We speak the plain truth" (2 Cor. 4:2, Phillips).

Paul recognized the effectiveness of the undiluted message. No tricks were needed. The Word of God is alive and powerful. It is relevant to life today. The other day on a flight to Pensacola, a Methodist layman seated mext to me said, "I believe the purpose of Sunday School is to teach the Bible and not something else." This confirmed again the fact that the message of God is effective in changing lives.

Proclaiming an undiluted message is necessary in the stewardship of the gospel. At a recent pastors' retreat in California, W. A. Carleton, professor, Golden Gate Baptist Theological Seminary, told an interesting story about the importance of honesty in Bible teaching.

He said that when his son, now a minister, was younger, he was highly impressed by a Training Union leader. From time to time the leader would demonstrate the effects of liquor on the human brain. He would secure the white of an egg and place it in a glass beaker. Then he would pour in liquor. In a few moments the egg white would become cloudy and harden. Years later when Dr. Carleton's son tried this experiment it never worked. In time the egg white would harden, but the effect was lost.

In time he saw his old Training Union leader and asked him about the demonstration. "Oh," said the leader, "You have to mix some turpentine in your liquor!"

Making his point, Dr. Carleton pointed out that it was not necessary to mix anything with the Word of God. The message of Christ must remain undiluted if it is to be effective in the lives of persons today.

The stewardship of the gospel demands that the message be interpreted in the light of today's experiences, but the undiluted message of God's Word is effective as it is. It must not be diluted by "another gospel" (2 Cor. 11:14).

Unselfish Ministry

Some time ago I was a visiting speaker in a church in another state. It was an anniversary celebration for the church, Homecoming Day. During the service the pastor took occasion to recognize everyone who had joined that church during the past year. He asked them to stand. There were about 200. He then asked them to come by the pulpit to be presented to the congregation. Without notes, and hesitating only once, he presented by name each new member to the congregation. I was amazed and deeply impressed. He knew the names of each of these new church members.

Following the service I asked him how he was able to remember everyone's first and last name. In an unassuming manner he said, "Oh, there is nothing to it if you love your people and are interested in them."

The secret of being caught up in this unselfish ministry is deep love and sincere interest. Once in possession of this treasure, the gospel of Christ, there is the immediate desire to share it with someone else.

Paul was a steward of the gospel. He proclaimed a message and lived a life in which Christ was central and dominant. His unselfish ministry led him to become the servant of others for Jesus' sake. In the text Paul spoke of himself as a willing servant of the Corinthians. There is no question but that he was glad for the privilege of being a servant of his Lord. He reflected this joy by becoming a servant to others. In obedience to Christ, he served others in preaching, teaching and pastoral care "for Jesus' sake" (2 Cor. 4:5).

The effect of an unselfish ministry in the stewardship of the gospel is illustrated in this survey of why people join a church.

5% choose a church because of the man in the pulpit.
9% choose a church because of the beauty of the building.

12% choose a church because of prior denominational affiliation.
22% choose a church because there were people in the church whom they respected.
34% choose a church because their neighbors and friends invited them.

—The *Biblical Recorder,* "A Personal Word" column by W. Perry Crouch

More people join our churches when we visit them. Visitation takes effort and reflects an unselfish spirit.

Another facet of this unselfish ministry is found in the experience of a teen-ager who spent a Saturday with a younger girl whose parents had left her at the county shelter. Neither the parents nor the grandparents of the girl wanted her. The teen-age friend packed a lunch, joining with other girls from her church, and went by bus to the zoo for a day of sightseeing, rides, and fun. She spent practically her entire savings from the past several weekly allowances! At the end of the day she told me, "I had a great time. It was cool to spend the day like this." Then she paused and in a moment reflected, "You know, my friend's parents don't even want her, but we had a good time. I spent almost all of my money, but it was worth it. My friend was so happy and so am I."

The late Chester Quarles, who was executive secretary-treasurer for Mississippi Baptists, illustrates the true spirit of unselfish ministry. On a trip to South America some years ago he carried a plastic briefcase with him. During the long flight he would ask the stewardesses to put ice inside inside the briefcase. When asked by a Baptist minister friend why he was doing that, he explained that he was taking polio vaccine to a missionary family in South America. There were small children in the family. The serum must be kept cold. He knew the importance of it. You see, he had polio as a child. He wanted to help the children of this missionary family if he could. It had not occurred to him that it was a bother.

Go—Tell

The Apostle Paul said that we preach Christ, not ourselves. Our work does not center in ourselves, but in Christ through our unselfish ministry.

Unequalled Master

In Mark 11, we read the account of Jesus' triumphant entry into Jerusalem. The time was near when he would face the ordeal of the cross.

You will recall that his disciples brought him a colt on which to ride. He rode into the city. The people rejoiced. Although there was a tinge of victory that day, the true victory had not yet been won. This came when our Master gave himself on the cross that we might become sons of God. He was and is the unequalled Master.

Read verses six and seven from the text: "For God, who commanded the light to shine out of darkness, hath shined in our hearts, to give the light of the glory of God in the face of Jesus Christ. But we have this treasure in earthen vessels, that the exellency of the power may be of God, and not of us."

Christ, the Master of men, is preeminent.

Andrew W. Blackwood, in his book, *Doctrinal Preaching for Today,* shares an illustration from life which points to Jesus as the unequalled Master. A number of years ago Charles R. Goff became pastor of the Methodist Temple in the downtown Chicago Loop area. Shortly after becoming pastor he felt the need of a Christian painting to impress the streams of visitors who visited the Temple. He arranged for an interview with Warner Sallman, whose "Head of Christ" now has a place of honor in the Temple. Fifty million copies of that painting have been made elsewhere. This is more than any other picture.

When the two men came together the artist astonished the minister by saying, "I have been waiting all these years to tell you that you gave me that picture. You gave Christ to me." It seems that years before, the minister had delivered at the Y.M.C.A. a number of Bible lectures. One of the lectures had impressed Sallman greatly. That night while asleep the artist saw a vision. It was the "Head of Christ." He awoke and made a sketch of what he had seen. From that drawing he later painted the picture which was placed in the Methodist Temple in Chicago.

Because someone "gave Christ to us," we now have the privilege of sharing Christ with others in the stewardship of the gospel.

No one may be compared to Jesus. He is Christ the Lord, the Son of God, the Savior of man.

Through our knowledge of him, we now can enlighten men because we can give them knowledge of the glory of God as we see it in the face of Jesus Christ.

As stewards of the gospel of Christ, ours is the privilege of sharing the light of the world with men who walk in darkness.

If you have flown over San Francisco Bay at night, you will recall the impressions you had about the vast darkness below. Bright lights line the edge of the bay and make their way up the valleys between the mountains, yet the bay itself is dark. Even with modern day ingenuity, we are incapable of lighting San Francisco Bay on a dark night. Yet a single flash of lightning will illumine the entire bay.

Similarly, God through us can enlighten those who walk in darkness. This is our stewardship of the gospel.

May it be that we will be undaunted messengers, preaching an undiluted message, providing an unselfish ministry and serving the unequalled Master.

11

When God Hits a Dry Well!

Wayne Dehoney

Text: Matthew 25:14–29.

Several years ago I was in a revival meeting at a church located in the heart of a great oil field. I stayed that week in the home of a "wildcatter." It was an exciting experience as he told of his life as an independent wildcatter who took the risks of surveying land, working up geological surveys, getting leases, financing, and drilling for oil.

I visited one of his "wildcat" wells where drilling was in progress. "It is going to be a gusher," he hoped. But it could be a "dry hole," only salt water or dry sand. After such an investment of labor and money, time, energy, skill, since—a dry hole!

That experience suggested my subject, "When *God* Strikes a Dry Well!" One of the most appalling questions that must fall on the mind of God is "Have I wasted the resources I invested in a man's life? I had such high hopes of a large return. But he has not produced for me in usefulness and service. I have hit a 'dry well'!"

What does God *do* when he strikes a dry well? In our text Jesus told a story which illustrates this very point. It is a parable in two acts.

The Parable

The central figure is the master. He owned a plantation, or vineyard. One day he decided to sell out and go into a far country. He disposed of his business and converted his assets into money.

Then there are these people who had worked for him, his servants, or more literally "slaves." He called in three of the servants and said, "You have worked with me a long time. I own everything; you own nothing. But I have been watching you. I believe you have ability and integrity. I am going to entrust you with the money I have gained from my property."

So he divided his money, to one servant five talents, to another two talents, another one talent. Talents, yes, a measure of *money!* A dollar, a pound, a shilling, a talent, they are synonymous. To one he gave $5,000; to another he gave $2,000; to another he gave $1,000. And he divided it according to their *several abilities.* So this is a story about the dispensing of money to servants, how they used that money, and the judgment of the master upon their use of that money.

Then the master took his journey, and the curtain comes down on Act One.

We immediately strike the parallel. First, God is the master, he owns all. Yes, we believe this. Our lives belong to him. All that we are, all that we have, all that we would be—our talents, our capacities, our abilities, our resources belong to God. *We* are his *resources.* God has investments in this world, and his investments are in people. We are his treasure.

Second, God is always studying us to find people whom he can trust. God is watching your life and my life, always looking—to find servants to whom he can commit more of his treasure. He is looking for those will be faithful stewards of opportunity, faithful stewards of talents, faithful stewards of capacities, faithful stewards of money, or faithful stewards of success.

Third, God gives to us according to our several abilities. He does not give equally. He gives to some five, and others two, and others one. Some people seem to be endowed with far more than others. But he does give to *all something.* This is exciting

When God Hits A Dry Well! 105

and encouraging to me. God has not left any of us without some endowment. God, the great giver, has invested something in all of our lives.

So, Jesus said the kingdom of heaven is like a master, giving out to several servants different proportions according to their several abilities, leaving an investment with them and saying, "Tend this. I trust you with it while I am away."

The curtain rises on Act Two. The master returns after a long interval. The servants have been left on their own. This is the way God does. He gives you the opportunity. He opens the door. He lets us see what we can do. He lets us try, and we are on our own. He does not stand over us and coerce us. But then, he returns—and he checks to see how we have done.

The servant who had received five talents—$5,000—the larger portion—said, "Look, Master, I have done well with what you gave me. I invested it. I used it. I multiplied it. Now I have doubled it." The master said, "Well done, thou good and faithful servant! I knew I could trust you. Now I will make you master over many things." The servant who had received two talents said, "Lord, I had two and I did the best I could with them. I have multiplied them and now there are two more." The master said, "Well done, thou good and faithful servant. You have been faithful, too, over a few things. Enter in to receive more. I will make you master over many things."

Now the attention focuses on the third servant, the one-talent man. "Lord, I did not have much. You gave him two, and you gave him five. You gave me only one. And I knew that you were a hard man and you reaped where you sowed not. I was afraid. I buried that talent in the ground and hid it to keep it safe, to be sure that nothing would happen to it."

Now, that was not unusual or unwise. In Jesus' day, it was more necessary to bury and hide one's treasure because there were no banks, no steel vaults, no security as we have today. So this was a very good way for the servant to hide his treasure to keep it safe. He said, "I protected it. I kept it. And, lo, I have it here"—and he brings the talent saying "I give it back to you, Master, kept safe."

The "Average" Person

From this point on, the focus of our story is on this one man. I think all of us can see ourselves as this one-talent man. We look around and see those who have so much more in every way—endowed with brilliance, training, culture, success, personality, talents. They can sing, speak, do this, do that, with ease and ability. We think, "Oh, what a talented dynamic person that is. But look at me—I'm just average. I'm so plain and ordinary."

I could have entitled this sermon, "The Perils of the Average Person"—the peril of being average, the peril of thinking that we are average; the peril of falling into this trap of saying, "I'm so average that I don't count! God is not depending upon me. God is going to move this kingdom along by the power of the five talent and the two talent people—but not through the likes of ordinary people like me." I want you to see what Jesus had to say about ordinary folks, ordinary talents, ordinary resources, ordinary abilities.

As I look at this man I see he is burdened with a sense of *inferiority*. Deep within all of us is this sense of inferiority. Even when we over-compensate; when we act so superior; when other people think we are really so adequate—deep inside we are saying, "I'm not adequate. I'm so insecure." Yes, we are insecure beings. God made us insecure in an insecure world—that we might ultimately find our security in him—not in ourselves. It is only human to see this fellow with his inferiority complex saying, "I don't have much. I don't count. My one talent is so little. What can I do for the Master?" Our Sunday School is full of folks who say that. Our church pews are full of folks who say that. The world is full of people saying, "I'm just so inferior." But I want you to understand that *God does not approve of this kind of self-effacing self-pity*. God has something to say to you and to me when we call ourselves ordinary and try to convince ourselves that we do not count. The servant said, "I only had *one* talent."

"And, Lord, I was afraid." Fear took over! Do you know

that kind of fear? Fear that is rooted in a sense of inadequacy? Do you know what it is to just face a situation and say, "I'm plain scared! I don't know how to cope with this. I am not adequate." That is the way the servant felt. He looked at this fellow with five talents who was wheeling and dealing, talking with bankers and real estate men. He seemed so at home in those circles. He saw the fellow with two talents, investing, trading, so sure of himself. But he said, "I was *afraid!*"

The master asked, "Why were you afraid?" "Oh, I was afraid I would *lose* what you gave me—if I lost it I knew you were a *hard man.*" Now that was a lie! The master was a *shrewd* man—but he was not a *hard* man. You see, we say to God, "Oh, God, the reason I don't do it—I might fail." The Lord answers, "What if you do fail?" "I'm afraid you'll do something to me if I fail."

Is God going to punish me when I do my best for him and then I do not succeed? The Scriptures repeatedly tell us that it is not *success* but *faithfulness* that is rewarded. God does not require that you succeed—but he does *demand* that you be *faithful.* We have a loving Father, not a *hard* Father. But the servant said, "I was afraid." I believe that this kind of unreasonable fear defeats the cause of God and the development of a Christian more than anything else in the world!

Remember when the children of Israel were ready to go in and occupy the Land of Promise. This great God had brought them out of bondage, had destroyed the armies of Pharaoh and opened the Red Sea before then. He brought then across the wilderness and fed them with manna from heaven. He guided them by a cloud of fire by night and a pillar of cloud by day. He brought them to the borders of the Promised Land and said, "Now, go in and conquer it. Take it. It is yours!"

They looked and saw giants in the land. Ten of the twelve spies returned and said, "They are so big and we are so small! We are as grasshoppers in their sight." They were afraid! They caused all the people to tremble and fear. Because of fear they went back into the wilderness for 38 years and wandered there until every last one of them had died before they could come in and claim the Promised Land.

How many times we look at the problems—and fail to see the great Problem-Solver who stands above us! No problem is beyond him, yet we focus on the problem; we focus on the giant; we focus on the difficulties. Fear takes over and we forget this great God who has gone with us; this God who stands with us; this God who says you can do it. The God who will give us the victory!

A soldier and his wife were traveling at sea. A storm came up and the soldier and his wife were on deck calmly watching the high waves. Another passenger, fear-stricken said, "How can you be so calm when our lives are in danger?" The soldier pulled his sword from the scabbard, put the point at his wife's throat and asked, "Are you afraid?" She quickly answered, "No." The soldier asked, "Why are you not afraid?" She smilingly replied, "Because the sword is in the hand of my husband. He loves me and I know that he cares for me."

The husband and soldier then returned the sword to the scabbard, turned to the man and said, "Sir, that's why I am not afraid either—for I know in whom I have believed, and am persuaded that he will keep that which I have committed unto him against that day. I have committed my life to Jesus Christ. His hand is on the sword."

The answer to fear is faith in a loving, caring Savior. It is just that simple!

What was the master's answer to the fearful one talented man? "Thou wicked and slothful servant!" What words! Now he could call him *slothful*. He could call him *lazy*. He could call him "no account." But he also calls him "wicked." "You are a wicked, wicked man!" This man had not *stolen* the money! He had not thrown it away in wild living! He had not *done* anything *wrong*! But the master called him wicked!

You do not have to murder to be wicked. You do not have to be a drunkard to be wicked. You do not have to be a gambler to be wicked. You do not have to be a wife-beater and child-deserter to be wicked. You can be a good, honorable, decent man who refuses to render a stewardship to God—and one day God will say, "You have been wicked. You have sinned. It will be held against you." Why? Because it is a sin not to take God seriously. What does the Scripture say? "To him that knoweth to do good, and doeth it not [if you know what is right and you do not do what is right] to him it is sin."

Do you know the *right* thing to do this morning? You say, "Deep in my heart, I know what I ought to do about teaching that Junior class . . . about witnessing. I know I ought to give my tithes to my church. But I have become afraid. I feel so inadequate. I am in debt. I am upset with someone in the church. But I know what I ought to do, and I do not do it." God says this will be accounted unto us as sin! "Thou wicked servant!"

The ninth chapter of John tells of a man born blind. One day in his darkness, he heard strange voices around him. A man by the name of Jesus was speaking. He heard Jesus clear his throat, spit on the ground. Then he felt the slimy touch of dust and spittle rubbed on his eyes. A strange voice said, "Son, now go, wash in the pool of Siloam." If you were that man, what would you have done? You say, "I would have obeyed, and been healed!" But would you? Would you have been healed? Or would you continue to sit there in your blindness? Have you obeyed the other commands of God? And received the blessings of obedience?

God says, "Bring ye all the tithes into the storehouse and prove me herewith sayeth the Lord." There is the command. The same as "Go now, wash in the pool of Siloam." And see if "I will not open up the windows of heaven and pour out a blessing." Do not say that you would have followed Jesus in faith in his day—unless you are willing, today, to obey him in faith also. Today Jesus still blesses those who will take him seriously! When he gives a command, when he makes a promise, and we obey, we receive the blessing of that promise.

Use or Lose

"Thou *wicked* servant! You did not *believe* me. You did not *do* what I said. You did not *obey* my command. Therefore, take from him that he hath and give it to another." That does not seem right! Take this one talent and give it to the man who has five? But that is the law of life. Either you *use*—or you *lose* what God has given you.

If I do not use my arm, I will lose it. Put this arm in a sling. Let me refuse to use it for six months and it will wither. It will lose its strength. Cover my eyes, block out the light. In time I will lose my sight. It is the same with faith—use it or lose it. You are not standing still; you are either going up the hill or down the hill in your Christian faith. Today you are either growing in faith, going up the hill or going down the hill, until one day you will have no faith.

This is true of prayer. Quit praying and you will lose the capacity to pray. But the more you pray the greater will be your power in prayer. The same is true of love. The more you love and forgive and understand, the more you have. Quit doing that and you lose the capacity to live, to forgive, to understand. This is the law of life. Use it, or lose it.

This is the law that God lays down for us regarding our material resources. And we are back to the parable of the talents—a parable about money. It is a parable on how you handle your possessions. This is Commitment Day—a time for you to take God seriously. Many of you did. Some have not. I beg you to take God seriously. For he is going to be serious with you one of these days! He will ask you to render a stewardship of the money he entrusted to you.

The tithe is the Lord's. Bring ye all the tithes into the storehouse. The storehouse is his church. And his church is marching today. The cause of Christ is being carried on the shoulders of these dedicated and wonderful people who are now making their commitment to tithe. March with them and God will bless you. Be a good steward of all that has given you—money and talent, abilities and time, and he will give you more.

12

In the Center of His Will

R. Earl Allen

In Baptist and other evangelical churches, the concept of a God-called pastor has always been basic. In recent years we are becoming more aware of God's call to laymen for evangelical witness where they are. Chaplains and servicemen, especially since World War II, have planted congregations abroad and in so-called "pioneer areas" of our own country.

One man, recently retired from the Army Corps of Engineers, together with his schoolteacher wife, organized several churches in the mountain and Pacific coast states. This was done in almost every place they were sent, unless they found a strong Southern Baptist Church nearby. A many-talented man, this engineer preached, led singing, visited, and built buildings. Such tentmakers, like Paul, spread the gospel in areas that might not otherwise be reached.

"Missions is simply trying to tell every man about God, who has made himself known through Jesus Christ, said Leslie Hill, missionary to the Philippines, speaking in Rosen Heights Baptist Church.

"Missions cannot be located by geographical position. Being a missionary is a spiritual condition," continued Mr. Hill. "An individual teaching school out in West Texas may be just as much a missionary as I am teaching in Mindanao Bible School in the Philippines. Especially if he knows in his heart God has said to him, 'This is the best use of your talents and at present this is where they are to be spent,' and if he is effectively witnessing for Christ in that place.

"But I could not go to a church in West Texas as pastor and be effective in this mission of God today," Mr. Hill said, "because, as I understand it, that is outside his will for my life. I will only be effective as I live in the center of his will. The matter of successful mission is not geographical location but the spiritual condition of a heart related to the will of God."

God has a place of service for all his people, and each Christian must find his own place, according to Mr. Hill.

That is true stewardship of vocation.

Stewardship is an interesting word. Many people limit its meaning and therefore do not really understand it.

"Steward" is an English term best defined as administrator, supervisor, or manager. It is used to translate two Greek words in the New Testament. One word means, basically, a man to whom the management of affairs is entrusted, such as an administrator, or one who has power of attorney. The other term carries the idea of house manager: one to whom was given responsibility of overseeing the various duties of the household, perhaps like a butler in a large establishment who has many servants under him.

Therefore the biblical idea of stewardship centers around managing or taking care of something which has been entrusted. It is a broad term, though many have narrowed it to only the financial realm. In so confining it, they certainly do not do justice to the biblical word.

The apostle Paul gave some general principles concerning the Christian and his life in 1 Corinthians 10:31 through 11:1. The kernel thought, in 10:31, is the injunction, "Whatsoever ye do, do all the glory of God." That covers all of life, everything—nothing is excluded. It is not something to be taken lightly. For our Christian life, the ramifications are far-reaching. Our deep realization of God's hold on us is necessary if our lives are to be useful for the Lord.

No matter what we do, we are to do it to the glory of God, Paul said. That includes our vocation. It applies to the field we have chosen, the means we have selected to support ourselves and our family. Our livelihood should be related to God.

Our lives are God-given. In Genesis 2:7 we find that "the Lord God formed man of the dust of the ground, and breathed into his nostrils the breath of life; and man became a living soul." We have been entrusted with our lives by the Lord.

Our lives are made up of time. Time is life and therefore it is important. God holds us responsible for how we use it. Most men spend at least forty hours a week at their job. That is approximately one-third of the time they are awake.

One-third of our life—that is how important our vocation is! But it is amazing how haphazardly some people choose their employment. They take the first thing that comes along and settle there permanently. Others choose their vocation with thought only of financial gain. Many go from job to job, vocation to vocation, playing a kind of bored "musical desks."

The general principle of seeking God's glory should govern the conduct of every hour of a Christian's life. Applied to the stewardship of our vocation, Paul's "whatsoever ye do" includes our work, that is, our choice of a job. It describes the way, the manner in which it should be pursued. It gives the goal—the witness, the influence we have on others.

The Work

What kind of work have you chosen for a life's vocation? Is it far-fetched to think that God uses a person in a particular secular job? No, that is part of a Christian's stewardship of life, according to the Bible.

Three distinct calls are made to men by God. First comes the call to repentance and salvation, second, the call to discipleship, and third, the call to some for special service. The first call goes out to all people, but many do not respond. The second call comes to those who are Christians and includes their vocation, for it concerns their stewardship in all areas of life. The third comes to certain Christians specially appointed to a particular work for God.

God intended men to work. Genesis 2:15 says, "And the Lord

God took the man, and put him into the garden of Eden to dress it and to keep it." In Exodus we find the familiar commandment, "Six days shalt thou labor, and do all thy work: But the seventh day is the sabbath of the Lord thy God" (20:9–10). Usually, we give major emphasis there to the command to observe the sabbath. But God also commands the activity of labor for the other six days.

Every individual needs to choose an occupation. This is of utmost importance to a Christian because he is steward of the life God has given him. "Moreover it is required in stewards, that a man be found faithful" (1 Cor. 4:2).

What should guide the Christian in this decision?

Henlee Barnette, in his book entitled *Has God Called You?*, gives some characteristics of Christian occupations. They are "(1) work which does a worthwhile job and meets a real need in society; (2) an occupation which enlists the best one has to offer in terms of gifts and skills; (3) work in which human beings are treated as persons and not as things, as 'thous' rather than 'its'; (4) work which requires of the worker integrity, creativity, imagination, love, and social usefulness; and (5) a job which one can pray about."

These characteristics ought to be brought home clearly to young people as they face this important decision. Our vocation is not strictly "our business." Certainly it is not outside the leadership of God. We are responsible to him for what we do with our time. The Christian should select his life's work on the basis of three questions: Will it be pleasing to the Lord? Will it help others? Will it be self-satisfying and rewarding?

But many make their decision to follow Christ after they are established in an occupation. These often encounter a time of real soul-searching. An experience with Christ does not automatically mean an individual has to change his vocation, but it does mean his life and its goals need to be reexamined in the light of his new commitment. That includes his occupation. The same three basic guidelines should be used. Sometimes one's conversion experience may dictate a change of vocation.

As Christian people, we need to be challenged by our work.

God can use the Christian layman as a lighthouse to others in his vocation. The best place to begin is when the occupation is chosen. Many jobs answer the listed characteristics, and through them we can find ways to influence our community for Christ.

George Beverly Shea, soloist for Billy Graham's crusades, is recognized around the world. In his autobiography, *Then Sings My Soul*, he tells of the vocational turning point in his life, entitling the chapter, "The Big Break I Didn't Take."

At the age of twenty-seven, he was working as a medical secretary for the Mutual Life Insurance Company in New York City. But singing was his avocation and his great joy. He had an opportunity to audition for the Lynn Murray Singers, described as "the Fred Waring group of that day." Waiting to sing for Mr. Murray, he learned that in addition to offering national radio exposure the job paid $75 a week—more than double what he was making.

After singing two numbers, he was given a piece of music to learn. One line made him uncomfortable: "and to hell with Burgundy." When he was a boy, his Wesleyan Methodist preacher father would have washed out his mouth with soap for saying something as strong as "shucks!"

He took the music with him, but that night he prayed about it. He thought of how he might hurt his father and his brothers who were in Christian work. He wondered what other compromises the job might lead to. "God, I don't know why You led me into this dilemma," he prayed. "Maybe You are trying to test me. But I can't believe this is the way You would have me serve You."

The next day his telephone rang. "Congratulations, Mr. Shea," Mr. Murray's secretary said. "You are now one of the Lynn Murray singers."

He swallowed hard and answered, "Thank you for the invitation, but I have decided I won't be able to accept the job. Please thank Mr. Murray for me and tell him I appreciate this kind offer."

One of Shea's friends took the job, and it led to other similar jobs. But that friend drifted further and further away from the church.

George Beverly Shea recognized God's hold on his life. He knew true stewardship demanded that his occupation please God. He did not fail the test, and God greatly honored him.

The Way

In the light of God's call, we must look not only at our choice of work but also at the way we perform it—how we conduct ourselves while pursuing it. "Whatsoever ye do, do all to the glory of God"—that is the way we are to do our work. That is why we must be concerned about our conduct.

The Christian is a new creature, a transformed individual. His testimony should echo Paul's: "I am crucified with Christ: nevertheless I live; yet not I, but Christ liveth in me; and the life which I now live in the flesh I live by the faith of the Son of God, who loved me and gave himself for me" (Gal. 2:20). This is how Christ can permeate every area of our life—including vocation. In this way God will be glorified.

This means that the Christian worker should get to work on time and not leave early. One who continually arrives late or habitually leaves before quitting time does not glorify God. The Bible says, "Thou shalt not steal," but many will steal a little time who would never dream of stealing money. We should give ourselves to our tasks with promptness and punctuality.

Stewardship of vocation will lead the Christian worker to be diligent at his job. Just putting in the required hours is not necessarily true stewardship of time in one's occupation. To glorify God we must do the best possible job. We must not work carelessly. "He also that is slothful in his work is brother to him that is a great waster" says Proverbs 18:9. We are also admonished in Romans 12:11 to be "not slothful in business." Proverbs 22:29 points out, "Seest thou a man diligent in his business? He shall stand before kings; he shall not stand before mean men."

Genuine stewardship of vocation should also be characterized by honesty. Many people see absolutely nothing wrong with taking a few small items from company stock. They carry things home for various reasons: pencils and paper for the childrens' school work, or a few pieces of hardware for a home project. If challenged, they shrug it off as a fringe benefit.

Most fringe benefits, however, are openly offered by the company. Small items are carried out on the sly. Such acts are costly to the employer. If a company employed forty thousand people and each of them took a pencil and small pad of paper three or four times a year, it would cost the company about twenty thousand dollars out the door. In the Old Testament, that comes under the injunction, "Thou shalt not steal." In the New Testament, Paul put it, "Whatsoever ye do, do all to the glory of God." Does taking things which belong to others glorify the Lord?

A final way in which your stewardship of vocation can be exercised to glorify God is your attitude on the job. No amount of diligence or honesty can make up for a bad attitude. Preciseness may satisfy your employer, but your attitude influences everyone around you. This goes back to the occupation's being self-fulfilling. If a job is approached in a resentful manner or with a bitter or bored attitude, God is not glorified.

What does it mean to glorify God? It means that we should exalt his holiness and majesty. As R. C. H. Lenski puts it, "We do all things for 'God's glory' when the excellence of God's attributes is made to shine forth by our actions so that men may see it."

Our God is a holy God. In both Leviticus 20:7 and 1 Peter 1:16 he commanded, "Be ye holy; for I am holy." We glorify God by being holy, by being sanctified, by being set apart. This covers every aspect of our lives—including our vocation. As a Christian layman if you take God with you to the job, you will find it makes the job easier, but most of all you will experience peace with God for a job well done.

Dr. Harry Ironside learned this in his youth. He worked for a shoemaker and part of his job was to prepare leather for soles. A piece of cowhide would be cut to size, soaked in water, and pounded with a flatheaded hammer until it was hard and dry. The task was tedious and of course young Harry wished it could be avoided.

At another shop down the block, Harry noticed their competitor did not pound the soles. He just soaked them and nailed them on immediately. One day young Ironside approached this man.

"I notice you put the soles on while they're wet," he said. "Are they just as good as if they were pounded?"

"No," the man replied with a wink and a cynical smile, "but they come back much quicker this way, my boy!"

The boy hurried back and suggested to his boss that maybe they were wasting their time drying out the leather so very carefully.

His Christian employer picked up his Bible. "Harry, I do not cobble shoes just for the money. I'm doing it for the glory of God." He read aloud Colossians 3:23, "And whatsoever ye do, do it heartily, as to the Lord, and not unto men."

He added soberly, "At the judgment seat of Christ, if I should have to view every shoe I've ever repaired, I would dread to have the Lord say, 'Dan, that was a poor job. You didn't do your best.' I want to see His smile and hear, 'Well done, good and faithful servant!'"

It was an object lesson in stewardship of vocation which Dr. Ironside never forgot.

The Witness

Genuine stewardship of vocation involves a witness. Every Christian represents God to those about him. Proper stewardship of life would dictate that such witness be the best possible at all times. That involves being a good witness for our Savior on the job.

"Give none offence," Paul said in 1 Corinthians 10:32–33, "neither to the Jews, nor to the Gentiles, nor to the church of God: Even as I please all men in all things, not seeking mine own profit, but the profit of many, that they may be saved."

First of all, "Give none offence." That can be translated, "be devoid of offence." Our lives should be so clear and faithful that no one will stumble in regard to the reality of God and the impact of the gospel. Others should not get a wrong impression of what a Christian is. The picture they get should be true and accurate.

We find in Romans 14:13, "Let us not, therefore, judge one another any more; but judge this, rather; that no man put a stumbling-block or an occasion to fall in his brother's way." First John 2:10 tells us, "He that loveth his brother abideth in the light, and there is none occasion of stumbling in him."

Pastors visiting prospects often hear something like, "Well, the church is full of hypocrites. Old Joe goes to church on Sunday, but you should see him at the office during the week! He tells such off-color stories you wouldn't think he ever went inside a church. If that's being a Christian, I want no part of it." Someone caused such a man to stumble. He cannot see Christ's love because of a fellow-worker's life. Some man has hurt the cause of his Lord by a poor witness.

Some people will be offended by our message that Christ died to save sinners. To be convicted of sin is unpleasant. But softening that message is not what Paul meant by "be devoid of offence." Someone has said, "Be very careful of the kind of life you lead; it may be the only Bible some people ever read." True stewardship of vocation demands a witness in action and word that measures up to God's standard.

"I please all men in all things," said Paul. But he did not mean that he compromised or gave up his convictions. We do not read far in Paul's letters before we realize that he was not a compromiser. He was a real defender of the faith, staunchly loyal to the gospel of Christ.

What *did* he mean? As he told the Galatians, he was crucified with Christ, who lived in him. Paul's concern was not that his own pride be defended, but that the good news be presented. He exalted his Lord. He had no time to worry over petty personal feelings; he was full of concern for others.

This is also involved in our stewardship of vocation. It is easy to compromise. It is easy to become "all things to all men" in a way that Paul did not mean. Many who on Sunday claim to be Christians act on the job as if they never heard of Christ and his life-changing message. Their speech and conduct do not show his influence.

Even more difficult is the matter of putting one's personal feelings out of the way. It is much easier to be on the defensive, to spend time guarding our own pride. To walk around with a chip on the shoulder does not glorify God, either. But to be concerned and interested in the feelings of others is a difficult assignment. We must do it just as Paul did it, by allowing Christ to live in us.

Paul stated his goal—the purpose of the witness of his life: "not seeking mine own profit, but the profit of many, that they may be saved." This was the central theme of all he did after his Damascus Road experience. What happened to him was so wonderful that he wanted everyone to have the same joy. Paul had a burning, passionate desire that never ceased until he drew his last breath.

That is stewardship of life and included in that is true stewardship of vocation. We are to be witnesses wherever we are and whatever we do. We are to glorify God with our words, our actions, our entire life. We are to let our light shine before men so that they may see Jesus in us.

The early disciples witnessed so aggressively that in just a few years they succeeded in creating quite a stir. In Acts 17:6, some people in Thessalonica said, "These that have turned the world upside down are come hither also." That is exactly what the world needs today—a turning upside down by the message of Christ.

The most effective way to do this is through the witness of laymen. One of the saddest developments in our churches has been the trend toward a clergy-only witness. Laymen are the key. A minister is expected to witness and share Christ, but when a layman does it the unsaved man can more easily identify. He realizes that the layman works in similar situations, but also cares enough to share his love for Christ.

That is what it is all about—sharing Christ with others. By dedicating all areas of life to the cause of Christ, the layman can be a responsible, vital witness for his Lord. Even on the job he can make great impact. God will be glorified, and by the grace of God, some will be saved.

The name of Heinz is known throughout the world for his "57 Varieties," especially pickles. After an evangelistic service, a minister turned and said to Mr. Heinz, "You're a Christian, but with all your energy, why aren't you up and at it for the Lord?" The great businessman went home in anger. That night he couldn't sleep. At 4 o'clock in the morning he was awake, praying that God would make him a true and zealous witness.

Not long afterward, at a meeting of bank presidents, Mr. Heinz turned to the man next to him and shared the joy he knew as a believer.

His friend looked at him in amazement. "I've wondered many times why, if you really believed in Christ, you never spoke to me about salvation." That man later became the first of 267 converts Mr. Heinz eventually influenced for Christ! He witnessed as he worked.

In *God's Gold Mines,* C. Roy Angell wrote about a bushman in Australia named Taylor who had reclaimed thousands of acres of desert by digging wells and irrigation ditches. He made green grass grow where hot sands once smothered all plant life.

"Why do you keep on living out in that hot desert?" someone asked him. "You're worth twenty-five million dollars. You have no need to labor any more. Why don't you take life a little easier?"

His answer was reminiscent of the apostle Paul. "God commissioned me just as he commissioned every missionary and preacher in the world," he declared. "He commissioned me to turn that desert into a beautiful place for people to live. I am not working for money, I am working for God. As long as he lets me work, I want to be turning the desert into green pastures."

It is the duty and privilege of every Christian to serve God wherever he is. When we realize that everything is God's and we are his stewards, the world will become a better place to live. Every Christian needs to make 1 Corinthians 6:20 his motto: "For ye are bought with a price: therefore glorify God in your body, and in your spirit, which are God's."